Praying
THROUGHOUT
THE DAY

A BOOK OF HOURS
FOR THOSE WITH ADDICTIONS

Harriet Roberts

Liguori
LIGUORI, MISSOURI

Imprimi Potest:
Thomas D. Picton, C.Ss.R.
Provincial, Denver Province
The Redemptorists

Published by Liguori Publications
Liguori, Missouri
www.liguori.org

Library of Congress Cataloging-in-Publication Data

Parker, Harriet Langdon Roberts.
    Praying throughout the day : a book of hours for those with addictions /
Harriet Roberts. — 1st ed.
        p.   cm.
    Includes bibliographical references.
    ISBN 978-0-7648-1479-2
    1. Recovering addicts—Religious life. 2. Addicts—Religious life. 3. Addicts
—Prayer books and devotions—English. 4. Divine office. I. Title.
    BL625.9.R43P37   2006
    242'.4—dc22   2006029817

The editor and publisher gratefully acknowledge permission to reprint/repro-
duce copyrighted works granted by the publishers/sources listed on pages
207–213.

Liguori Publications, a nonprofit corporation, is an apostolate of the Redemptorists. To learn more about the Redemptorists, visit *Redemptorists.com*.

Printed in the United States of America
11 10 09 08 07   5 4 3 2 1
First edition

CONTENTS

TO THE MEMORY
OF MY PARENTS

ACKNOWLEDGMENTS

Thanks go first to Evelyn and Jim Whitehead. Were it not for Evelyn's inspired and timely leap, this book would not exist. Thank you for your generosity and belief in this journey.

I am grateful to faithful friends who offered, at different times, exactly what was needed: Reverend F. Dean and Beverly Lueking, consummate "shepherds," whose sheep know they have been entertained by angels. Lois Catrambone, truly the apple of God's eye. Daniel Busch, a constant encouragement and sure guide. Steve and Rena Cutright, practitioners of sacred friendship.

Marge Chesney goes quietly forth as Christ's emissary to this world, watching, listening, caring, and giving. Mim Halter radiates God's love more than she can know. Richard Hillert transforms the ordinary into a feast. David Heim and Barbara Hofmaier exemplify the triumph of the human spirit, which comes from allowing ourselves to find our place in God's plan.

Cheryl Spooner gave me the gift of telling the truth. Linda Thomas graciously provided insight at a pivotal point in the writing. Mary Jo Hubick deepened my understanding of how addictive thinking is transmitted through generations. Stephen Schmidt, Bill Schmidt, and Paul Giblin offered new opportunities to explore the intertwining of addiction and depression. Dick Schwartz decoded the parts, which are the keys to the puzzle.

At Liguori, thanks go especially to Danny Michaels, the midwife of this endeavor, who, with Judy Ahlers, shaped this project with patience and creativity.

Finally, my deepest thanks to John, Catherine, and Daniel, the embodiment of "life in abundance," whose affirming love allowed the ideas in this book to germinate, grow in many directions, and finally take shape, pruned and useful.

HARRIET ROBERTS

INTRODUCTION

I came that [you] might have life, and have it abundantly.
JOHN 10:10

This book is meant for those who have been touched by
addiction, which is everyone. It is meant as a practical guide
to progressing through the hours of an ordinary day, with
predictable periods of rest and prayer. It is not a "how to" for
addiction recovery, and it does not endorse any particular
recovery style or program.

Its focus is on developing a relationship between God
and the reader to a point the Benedictines call "preferring
Christ" to all else the world has to offer. To create a deep
and lasting relationship with anyone you need to have
time to spend together, curiosity about the other person,
respect, and a love that transcends what we "like." Within
the therapeutic community, it is coming to be recognized
that healing occurs not so much from the particular theory
or "technique" that is used, but from the relationship that
is established between the participants. Rumi, the Persian
poet, spoke to this phenomenon:

> *Miracles don't cause faith,*
> *but rather the scent of kindredness*
> *that unites people.*
> *Miracles overwhelm unbelief.*
> *Faith grows from friendship.*
> RUMI

This book is written from an ecumenical Christian perspective and includes prayers, hymns, canticles, stories, poems, and responses from a variety of sources. You are encouraged to read the selections in any way that has meaning for you: as divinely inspired Scripture, history, literature, allegory, or metaphor, and to insert yourself into the stories. We are a flawed humanity, which is brilliantly clear when we meet the characters who populate the biblical narratives. This is one place for us to begin to know God's promises, angers, frustrations, loves, jealousies, and the lavish forgiveness that he is willing to grant his wayward people, us. As we meet these personalities, we will recognize ourselves, along with all the drives, desires, longings, loneliness, selfishness, grandiosity, impetuousness, generosity, laziness, shallowness, manipulativeness, and prejudices that come with being human.

This *Book of Hours* adapts the concept of "fixed-hour" prayer, which dates back to the Romans, and was refined in the Benedictine monastic communities, to the process of recovery for persons struggling with addictions—their own or someone else's.

Recovery programs encourage their participants to take things "one day at a time," but time is a relative concept and the experience of "one day" can vary from person to person. Common to all perspectives, however, is the understanding that "one day" is a discrete unit of time. From the viewpoint of someone wrestling with addiction, an unbroken stretch of twelve to twenty-four hours can seem infinite, but it might not seem so daunting when divided into smaller units. In other words, using a visual metaphor, instead of anticipating the day as a journey down the entire length of a long, unbroken "clothesline," the traveler could, instead, think of "one day" as a "fence" with periodic, predictable guideposts to uphold and sustain the traveler, while providing a realistic gauge against which to measure his or her progress.

The ancient spiritual practice divides twenty-four hours into three-hour segments, producing eight designated "hours," specific times during the day when all work comes to a halt and the entire community, monastic or otherwise, gathers together for prayer. It is suggestive of the action of satellite instruments today, which periodically and automatically recalibrate against an "absolute" clock. It also develops a habit of prayer that reaches deep into the heart of the believer to establish a more intimate connection to God. It can change the nature of our communication with God from a static, specific event of asking for what we need, to an ongoing conversation that helps us learn how to realign our will with God's will.

The hours are named according to their position on the clock. Starting at 6:00 AM is *prime* (first hour), then *terce* (third hour) at 9:00 AM, *sext* (sixth hour) at noon, *nones* (ninth hour) at 3:00 PM, and *vespers* at 6:00 PM. *Compline* ends the day at 9:00 PM. This liturgy uses four of these hours, spaced six hours apart, with the exception of final prayer, which comes after three hours, at 9:00 PM.

Within the format of *The Liturgy of the Hours*, the person can focus his or her energy and attention on a three-hour segment at a time, knowing he or she will receive periodic spiritual refreshment from readings, hymns, and prayers, and from other pilgrims (the desert fathers and mothers, the saints, and all the faithful) who have, whether addicted or not, traveled this road before.

Traditionally, the content of each "hour" follows a standard sequence: Invitatory, Hymn, Antiphon, Psalm, repeated Antiphon, Reading, Response, and Concluding Prayer. During Compline, there may be alterations or additional opportunities for reflection. In this liturgy, readings, prayers, hymns, and canticles have been compiled for Prime (Morning Prayer), Sext (Midday Prayer), Vespers (Evening Prayer), and Compline (Night Prayer), with each prayer hour oriented around a common, problematic theme or issue within the life of addiction; examples would be safety, "demons," idols, blame, forgiveness, interdependence, denial and rationalization, the grip of addiction, relapse, loss, and ultimate triumph.

The framework for this fourteen-day liturgy is designed as follows. Each day concentrates on one of the fourteen stations of the cross (events of Christ's passion and death). The addiction issues, listed at the beginning of each day's prayers, are topics applicable to stages of change, as suggested by the subject of each station, with specific reference to addiction.

The reader is strongly encouraged to read only one hour at a time, and one day at a time. The material is fairly dense and will become overwhelming if it is read as a continuous narrative.

One of the great barriers to healing is the problem of *access*. Often, addicted persons are too numbed to know what they think or feel, or they cannot connect that information with their "feeling center," which tells them what it means. Perhaps they don't know *what* to pray, or *how* to express the pain of separation from everything meaningful to them, especially from the God who breathes in each of us and resides in our deepest space. And, sometimes we need others to pray for us, to express the inexpressible. Who better to do that than the inspired voices of the faithful?

As addiction selectively numbs parts of the person, it also distorts *time* and *space*, and plays havoc with one's conception of reality. Here an external structure, or "scaffolding," can be helpful. The goal is to help the traveler create a sacred *space*, where the underlying issues of the illness can rise to the surface and be examined in safety. Deception, both of self and others, often makes this process dangerous or impossible outside the safe context of prayer.

By using *The Liturgy of the Hours* as a tool of measurement, to create *space* and demarcate *time* into rational, objective, and predictable units, we begin to establish a flow of rhythmic and reciprocal conversation within ourselves and with God. Meditation on the rosary comes to mind, and Muslim prayer beads; in popular culture, the astonishing success of the disc "Chant" speaks to the deep need people have for the slow and rhythmic movement of prayer.

If *space* and *time* can be brought into healthy, realistic alignment, then a person can move on to approach the actual substance of the addiction. Tethered to a framework, the fear of "falling" diminishes. Gradually, gaining insight revealed through the texts, the person realizes that he or she is not just addressing the addiction(s), but practicing how to bring one's whole self to the meditation, and through prayer, healing can take place.

MORNING PRAYER

For those struggling with addiction, the beginning of a new day is often accompanied by trepidation and acute anxiety. Perhaps it is fear of criticism, because one is so emotionally fragile, or has anxiety about doing one's job well—or even at all; or maybe it's shame for not even being able to get out of bed. Joy and satisfaction seem out of reach in this micro-universe. The hymn text offers hope:

HYMN   *Lord of All Hopefulness (v. 1)*

Lord of all hopefulness, Lord of all joy,
Whose trust, ever childlike, no cares could destroy,
Be there at our waking, and give us, we pray,
Your bliss in our hearts, Lord, at the break of the day.

MIDDAY PRAYER

It's noon, time for lunch, and a little rest, maybe. Here, it is easy to lose track of the big picture, to hyperfocus on an aspect of work or personal relationships and forget that to live the abundant life God has for us we must maintain a balance—physically, emotionally, psychologically, and spiritually. It is easy, right now, to slip back into the addictive substance or behavior. Whether that happens or not, we wonder if we're making progress:

> *A monk was once asked,*
> *"What do you do up there in the monastery?"*
> *He replied, "We fall and get up,*
> *fall and get up, fall and get up again."*
> SEEKING GOD BY ESTHER DE WAAL

EVENING PRAYER

This hour's danger lies in our vulnerability. Hungry and tired, we are most tempted when our defenses are at their lowest point. We try to trick ourselves. If we're alone, "Who's going to know if I have just one drink? Of course, it will be only one." Truth says otherwise. Self-deception is our constant companion. What to do?

Home with a young family, instead of relaxing after a long day, we often experience this part of the day as the busiest. Everyone is running in different directions, all on different timetables. No one is doing what anyone else is doing: "Why do they schedule Little League over the dinner hour?" We console ourselves with something sweet, on the run, "A few cookies will do, in place of dinner." And then maybe a few more. We feel alone, disconnected. The Lord said to Jeremiah, "Do not be afraid...for I am with you to deliver you, says the LORD" (Jeremiah 1:8).

NIGHT PRAYER

For the addicted person, rest is often hard to come by. There may be difficulty falling asleep, staying asleep. Chemical substances may play a part, or guilt brought on by judging our productiveness today—what we have done and what we have left undone. Within our restlessness, the body betrays us. No matter our fatigue, the stress hormones we need for "fight or flight" peak at 4:00 AM, waking us, and for the addicted person, that's the beginning of the new day.

Addiction is rampant in our society. The question, now, is how can we use the ancient and proven disciplines of contemplative prayer, a rhythm of pray, work, study, rest, and other monastic practices, to foster reconnection with God, and through that process, bring about the healing of illness, spirit, mind, and body.

In John 5:6, Jesus asks the paralyzed man at the pool at Bethesda, "Do you want to get well?" That question is extremely important in the healing of addictions, because if you do not really desire wholeness, any attempt at recovery will be futile. Why would anyone not want to get well? One man said that the cure was worse than the disease.

Another reason could be that we complain, but we quickly become comfortable with our "demons"; they provide us with some kind of seen or unseen protection from whatever is assaulting our spirits and overwhelming us. Perhaps the pain of the attack is too intense; we *need* those demons and will not be able to part with them until we are thoroughly committed to recovery, by replacing the addictive substances or behaviors with an intimate, vibrant, and deepened relationship with God. Change is hard, uncomfortable, demanding, and it shows us things about ourselves that maybe we'd rather not see. But, those hesitations must be coupled with our innate flexibility and ability to change: It is *never* too late. We *always* have a choice.

Recovery is not linear, and some lose patience with the addicted person who relapses after one attempt. There are many false starts, and success and relapse cohabit until, with God's help, willingness to change takes the upper hand.

It involves personal commitment to "our Lord's perverse ethic of vulnerability, and gain through loss."

The process of recovery is similar to the process of peeling an onion. From the exterior, we make certain assumptions about the underlying onion, but once we begin peeling back the layers, it is obvious that we will need to alter our plan of action to maximize the amount of "healthy" onion we can recover. Layers are of different sizes and thickness, not always (actually, never) perfectly aligned. They attach to each other, and the intermediate membranes rip, stick, and generally complicate the process. Then there is also the unpleasant side effect of causing us to cry. So it is with the complex, baffling, intransigent aspects of addiction, and recovery from it.

Addiction is not the problem itself. It is the symptom of a deeper problem that, for whatever reason, has not yet been successfully worked through. To hide the cookies or pour the sherry down the drain may give someone momentary satisfaction, but it will not halt the drive that is hiding behind the symptom.

Addiction, and the effects of addiction, touch everyone: adults, children, families, friends, teachers, coworkers, and clergy; and it can affect every aspect of our lives: physical, mental, emotional, spiritual, financial, cognitive, interpersonal. It attacks our self-esteem, our sense of competence, our ability to love. It is not "us against them"…because we are all "them." We are all diminished by addiction, in one way or another.

If it is true that our DNA programs us to need exercise for a physically healthy life, then there must be a corollary truth for our mental, emotional, and spiritual well-being. I believe those ancient monastics understood it and practiced it. An orderly progression through each day, alternating prayer, work, rest, and study. If that rhythm seems like an outrageous impossibility when we consider our own hectic lives, then perhaps we need to consider them more closely. The assault of our modern lifestyles on those deeper aspects of our selves which, under enough pressure, give in to addiction or wither altogether is alarming in its implications. We can do it all, but at what cost? Addiction, which erodes the human soul even further? Wouldn't it be better to work at prevention than at repair?

There are many people struggling to live a prayerful and meaningful life, so almost anyone can find this book useful—whether you are fighting an addiction, living or working with someone who is, or are an unknowing victim of "addictive thinking" that has filtered through the generations in your family, even where no active addiction is present. Take some time to establish a rhythm of prayer for yourself; you will know when you find the right pace and reach the appropriate depth *for you*. My prayer for you would echo Simeon's song (see Luke 2:29–32) when he realized that the infant Jesus was, in fact, the long-awaited Messiah, Immanuel, God with us:

Lord, now let your servant go in peace;
   your word has been fulfilled.
My own eyes have seen the salvation
   which you have prepared
   in the sight of every people:
a light to reveal you to the nations and
   the glory of your people Israel.

NUNC DIMITTIS

to which we add:

Glory to the Father, and to the Son, and to
the Holy Spirit, as it was in the beginning,
is now, and will be forever. Amen.

STATION 1 ~ *Jesus is condemned to die*

ADDICTION ISSUES ~ *Denial, isolation, betrayal*

 MORNING PRAYER

INVITATION TO PRAYER

O Lord, open my lips and my mouth will declare your praise. Cleanse my heart of any worthless, evil, or distracting thoughts. Give me the wisdom and love to pray with attention, reverence, and devotion. Father, let my prayer be heard in your presence, for it is offered through Christ our Lord. Amen.

HYMN   *Morning Has Broken*

Morning has broken, like the first morning
Blackbird has spoken, like the first bird
Praise for the singing, praise for the morning
Praise for the springing fresh from the world

Sweet the rain's new fall, sunlit from heaven
Like the first dewfall, on the first grass
Praise for the sweetness of the wet garden
Sprung in completeness where his feet pass

Mine is the sunlight, mine is the morning
Born of the one light, Eden saw play
Praise with elation, praise every morning
God's recreation of the new day

ANTIPHON   *Psalm 5:3*

O LORD...you hear my voice;
    in the morning I plead my case to you, and watch.

As the deer longs for flowing streams,
    so my soul longs for you, O God.
My soul thirsts for God,
    for the living God.
When shall I come and behold
    the face of God?
My tears have been my food
    day and night,
while people say to me continually,
    "Where is your God?"…

Deep calls to deep
    at the thunder of your [waterfalls];
all your waves and your billows
    have gone over me.…

I say to God, my rock,
    "Why have you forgotten me?
Why must I walk about mournfully,
    because the enemy [addictive substances and behaviors]
        oppresses me?"
As with a deadly wound in my body,
    my adversaries [addictive substances and behaviors]
        taunt me,
while they say to me continually,
    "Where is your God?"

Why are you cast down, O my soul,
    and why are you disquieted within me?
Hope in God; for I shall again praise him,
    my help and my God.

PRAYER TO CARRY WITH ME   *Psalm 5:3*

O LORD, in the morning you hear my voice; / in the morning
I plead my case to you, and watch.

READING   *John 4:7, 9–14*

A Samaritan woman came to draw water, and Jesus said to
her, "Give me a drink." The Samaritan woman said to him,
"How is it that you, a Jew, ask a drink of me, a woman of Samaria?"…Jesus answered her, "If you knew the gift of God,
and who it is that is saying to you, 'Give me a drink,' you
would have asked him, and he would have given you living
water." The woman said to him, "Sir, you have no bucket and
the well is deep. Where do you get that living water? Are you
greater than our ancestor Jacob, who gave us the well, and
with his sons and flocks drank from it?" Jesus said to her,
"Everyone who drinks of this water will be thirsty again, but
those who drink of the water that I will give them will never
be thirsty. The water that I will give will become in them a
spring of water gushing up to eternal life."

RESPONSE   *Revelation 7:17*

…the Lamb…will be their shepherd,
    and he will guide them to springs of [living water].

READING   *John 7:37–38*

…while Jesus was standing there, he cried out, "Let anyone who is thirsty come to me, and let the one who believes
in me drink. As the scripture has said, 'Out of the believer's
heart shall flow rivers of living water.' "

RESPONSE

Where can *I* find this living water? Among God's gifts to me,
where do I look to find this "new life"?

ACTION

Today, I will pay close attention to who or what kills my body and spirit, and to who or what opens my body and spirit to new life.

CONCLUDING PRAYER

Each morning is a new beginning of our life.
  Each day is a finished whole.
The present day marks the boundary
  of our cares and concerns.
It is long enough to find God or to lose him,
  to keep faith,
  or fall into disgrace.
God created day and night for us so we need not
  wander without boundaries, but may be able
  to see in every morning
  the goal of the evening ahead.
Just as the ancient sun rises anew every day,
  so the eternal mercy of God is new every morning.
Every morning God gives us
  the gift of comprehending anew
  his faithfulness of old;
  thus, in the midst of our life with God,
  we may daily begin a new life with him.
The first moments of the new day are for
  God's liberating grace,
  God's sanctifying presence.
Before the heart
  unlocks itself for the world,

God wants to open it for himself;
  Before the ear takes in
  the countless voices of the day,
  it should hear in the early hours
  the voice of the
  Creator and Redeemer.
God prepared the stillness
  of the first morning for himself.
It should remain his.

DIETRICH BONHOEFFER

 ## MIDDAY PRAYER

INVITATION TO PRAYER

O God of mercy, I call to you; let your face shine upon me, and hold me in your steadfast love (see Psalm 31:16–17). Give me confidence in my work and my worth, so that I might use my energy in positive and creative ways, and not deplete it with temporary satisfactions that sap my energy and make me ashamed. Help me to build, or recover a strong foundation, built on the rock of your love, not on the shifting sands of instant gratification. I am strong, Lord, but in ways I don't understand, I derailed and lost my focus. I forget that I have the power to change or leave what is toxic to my spirit. Remind me of my strength, and that it all comes from you. Help me to reclaim my energy and my life. Amen.

HYMN *There Is a Balm in Gilead*
Refrain
There is a balm in Gilead to make the wounded whole;
  there is a balm in Gilead to heal the sin sick soul.

Sometimes I feel discouraged and think my work's in vain,
  but then the Holy Spirit revives my soul again.

Refrain

If you cannot preach like Peter, if you cannot pray like Paul,
  you can tell the love of Jesus, and say, "He died for all."

Refrain

Don't ever feel discouraged, for Jesus is your friend;
  and if you lack for knowledge he'll ne'er refuse to lend.

Refrain

ANTIPHON   *Psalm 138:6*
For though the LORD is high,
he [looks upon] the lowly...

PSALM   *Psalm 13*
How long, O LORD? Will you forget me forever?
  How long will you hide your face from me?
How long must I bear pain in my soul,
  and have sorrow in my heart all day long?
How long shall my enemy be exalted over me?

Consider and answer me, O LORD my God!
  Give light to my eyes, or I will sleep the sleep of death,
and my enemy will say, "I have prevailed";
my foes will rejoice because I am shaken.

But I trusted in your steadfast love;
  my heart shall rejoice in your salvation.
I will sing to the Lord,
  because he has dealt bountifully with me.

Prayer to Carry With Me
Psalm 138:6

For though the LORD is high, he [looks upon] the lowly…

Reading
Folk Tale

An elderly woman had two large water pots hung at either end of a pole she carried across her neck. One pot was perfect, but the other was cracked. Daily, at the end of her walk from the stream to the house, the cracked pot was only half full.

Her neighbor praised her one fine pot, but said the other was an embarrassment because of its imperfection, only able to do half the work it was meant to do. Some time later her neighbor, realizing the woman had no intention of fixing the crack, spoke again.

"You should be ashamed that the crack in your pot causes it to leak water all the way back to your house."

The old woman answered, "Did you notice there are flowers on one side of the path, but not the other? I have always known about the crack in my pot, so I planted flower seeds there, and every day on our walk back from the stream, my pot waters them. Without my pot being just the way it is, there would not be this beauty to grace our lives."

Response
I am enough.

Reading
Matthew 11:28–30

"Come to me, all you that are weary and are carrying heavy burdens, and I will give you rest. Take my yoke upon you, and learn from me; for I am gentle and humble in heart, and you will find rest for your souls. For my yoke is easy, and my burden is light."

RESPONSE

"The LORD, the LORD,
a God merciful and gracious,
slow to anger,
and abounding in steadfast love and faithfulness…"

ACTION

Today I will pay close attention to who or what kills my body and spirit, and to who or what opens my body and spirit to new life.

CONCLUDING PRAYER

Lord, you have made us weak, so that we might know your strength. You have made us indecisive, so that we might know your unwavering faithfulness. Jesus says, "I am the way, the truth, and the life." Give us strength for the journey and steadfast confidence in your presence beside us. Amen.

 EVENING PRAYER

INVITATION TO PRAYER

Lord Jesus, you invite us to life and give us the gift of ourselves. But often we feel the need to improve upon the very self you gave us, an indestructible soul with an infinite capacity to hold your love. But instead, we fill it with noise, motion, and all the baubles of the world that beckon us and promise to make us "better." And then there is no more room for you, or us. Draw us close, and remind us that, in you, we are already "better." Amen.

HYMN

Evening Prayer (Vespers)

Jesus Christ is the Light of the world,
    the light no darkness can overcome.

Stay with us, Lord, for it is evening,
    and the day is almost over.
Let your light scatter the darkness,
    and illumine your church.

Joyous light of glory:
    of the immortal Father;
    heavenly, holy, blessed Jesus Christ.
We have come to the setting of the sun,
    and we look to the evening light.
We sing to God, the Father, Son, and Holy Spirit:
    You are worthy of being praised
    with pure voices forever.
Son of God, O Giver of life:
    the universe proclaims your glory.

ANTIPHON   *Psalm 27:14*

Wait for the LORD;
    be strong, and let your heart take courage;
wait for the LORD!

PSALM   *Psalm 27:1–4, 7–9*

The LORD is my light and my salvation;
    whom shall I fear?
The LORD is the stronghold of my life;
    of whom shall I be afraid?

When evildoers assail me
    to devour my flesh—
my adversaries and foes—
    they shall stumble and fall.
Though an army encamp against me,
    my heart shall not fear;

though war rise up against me,
    yet I will be confident.

One thing I asked of the LORD,
    that I will seek after:
to live in the house of the LORD
    all the days of my life,
to behold the beauty of the LORD,
    and to inquire in his temple.

Hear, O LORD, when I cry aloud,
    be gracious to me and answer me!
"Come," my heart says, "seek his face!"
    Your face, LORD, do I seek.
    Do not hide your face from me.

PRAYER TO CARRY WITH ME   *Psalm 27:14*
Wait for the LORD;
    be strong and let your heart take courage;
wait for the LORD!

READING   *Matthew 26:31, 33–35, 49, 69–75*
…Jesus said to them [at dinner], "You will all become
deserters because of me this night; for it is written,

  'I will strike the shepherd,
      and the sheep of the flock will be scattered.' "

…Peter said to him, "Though all become deserters because
of you, I will never desert you." Jesus said to him, "Truly I
tell you, this very night, before the cock crows, you will deny
me three times." Peter said to him, "Even though I must die
with you, I will not deny you.…"

    Then they came and laid hands on Jesus and arrested him.…

Now Peter was sitting outside in the courtyard [of the high priest, Caiaphas]. A servant-girl came to him and said, "You also were with Jesus the Galilean." But he denied it before all of them, saying, "I do not know what you are talking about." When he went out to the porch, another servant-girl saw him, and she said to the bystanders, "This man was with Jesus of Nazareth." Again, he denied it with an oath, "I do not know the man." After a little while, the bystanders came up and said to Peter, "Certainly you are also one of them, for your accent betrays you." Then he began to curse and swore an oath, "I do not know the man!" At that moment the cock crowed. Then Peter remembered what Jesus had said: "Before the cock crows, you will deny me three times." And he went out and wept bitterly.

RESPONSE

Peter paid dearly for his impetuous overconfidence. Do we promise more than we can deliver, because what we *can* offer doesn't seem good enough?

ACTION

Today I will pay close attention to who or what kills my body and spirit, and to who or what opens my body and spirit to new life.

CONCLUDING PRAYER

Lord…protect me from the impetuous desires of my nature—to eat and drink too much, to offer grandiose promises, to be careless with my resources: money, time, and energy, emotional, physical, and spiritual. Take away my fear of what is real. Teach me to recognize your greatest gift to me, the wholeness of my self. Hold me in your light, so that I can see myself as you see me. Amen.

INVITATION TO PRAYER

O God of refuge, draw our tired and broken souls to you.
Protect us from our anxiety over everything that pursues
us and keeps us from you. In the space I make for you in my
heart, meet me, hold me. Let me never forget your strength,
your love, and your infinite forgiveness. Amen.

HYMN   *Stay With Us*

Stay with us, Lord Jesus,
Stay with us.
Stay with us, it soon is evening,
And night is falling.

Jesus Christ, the world's true light!
Shine so the darkness cannot overcome it!
Stay with us, Lord Jesus, it soon is evening,
Stay with us, Lord Jesus, for night is falling.
Let your light pierce the darkness
And fill your church with its glory.

Stay with us, Lord Jesus,
Stay with us,
Stay with us, it soon is evening,
And night is falling.

SILENT REFLECTION ON THE DAY AND ON OURSELVES

ANTIPHON   *Deuteronomy 20:3*

"Do not lose heart, or be afraid...."

PSALM

Protect me, O God, for in you I take refuge.
I say to the LORD, "You are my Lord;
  I have no good apart from you."

I bless the LORD who gives me counsel;
  in the night also my heart instructs me.
I keep the LORD always before me;
  because he is at my right hand, I shall not be moved.

Therefore my heart is glad, and my soul rejoices;
  my body also rests secure.
For you do not give me up to [the grave],
  or let your faithful one see the Pit.

You show me the path of life.
  In your presence there is fullness of joy;
  in your right hand are pleasures forevermore.

PRAYER TO CARRY WITH ME   *Deuteronomy 20:4*

"Do not lose heart, or be afraid.…"

READING   *John 21:15–19*

…Jesus said to Simon Peter, "Simon son of John, do you love me more than these?" He said to him, "Yes, Lord; you know that I love you." Jesus said to him, "Feed my lambs." A second time he said to him, "Simon son of John, do you love me?" He said to him, "Yes, Lord; you know that I love you." Jesus said to him, "Tend my sheep." He said to him the third time, "Simon son of John, do you love me?" Peter felt hurt because he said to him the third time, "Do you love me?" And he said to him, "Lord, you know everything; you know that I love you." Jesus said to him, "Feed my sheep." Very truly, I tell you, when you were younger, you used to fasten your own belt and to go wherever you wished. But when you grow old…someone else will fasten a belt around you and take you where you do not wish to go.…After this he said to him, "Follow me."

RESPONSE   *Romans 6:23*

For the wages of sin is death, but the free gift of God is eternal life.

SILENT PRAYER FOR THE WORLD, OTHERS, AND OURSELVES

ACTION

Today I have paid close attention to what kills my body and spirit, and to what opens my body and spirit to new life.

CONCLUDING PRAYER   *Our Father*

Our Father, who art in heaven, hallowed be thy name;
   thy kingdom come, thy will be done on earth as it is in
   heaven.
Give us this day our daily bread; and forgive us our
   trespasses, as we forgive those who trespass against us;
and lead us not into temptation, but deliver us from evil.
   For the kingdom, the power, and the glory are yours
   now and for ever. Amen.

STATION 2 ~ *Jesus carries his cross*

ADDICTION ISSUES ~ *Rationalization, truth,*
forgiveness

 MORNING PRAYER

INVITATION TO PRAYER

O Lord of hope, open my lips and my mouth will declare
your praise. Cleanse my heart of any worthless, evil, or
distracting thoughts. Give me the wisdom and love necessary to pray with attention, reverence, and devotion. Father,
let my prayer be heard in your presence, for it is offered
through Christ our Lord. Amen.

HYMN   *Lord of All Hopefulness (v. 1)*

Lord of all hopefulness, Lord of all joy,
Whose trust, ever childlike, no cares could destroy:
Be there at our waking, and give us, we pray,
Your bliss in our hearts, Lord, at the break of the day.

ANTIPHON   *Psalm 95:7*

…he is our God,
   and we are the people of his pasture,
   and the sheep of his hand.

PSALM   *Psalm 95:1–7*

O come, let us sing to the LORD;
   let us make a joyful noise to the rock of our salvation!
Let us come into his presence with thanksgiving;
   let us make a joyful noise to him with songs of praise!

For the LORD is a great God,
    and a great King above all gods.
In his hand are the depths of the earth;
    the heights of the mountains are his also.
The sea is his, for he made it,
    and the dry land, which his hands have formed.

O come, let us worship and bow down,
    let us kneel before the LORD, our Maker!
For he is our God,
    and we are the people of his pasture,
    and the sheep of his hand.

O that today you would listen to his voice!

PRAYER TO CARRY WITH ME   *Isaiah 43:5*
"Do not fear, for I am with you."

READING   *John 11:1–3, 6–7, 11, 17, 23–27,*
                               32–35, 38–39, 41, 43–44

Now a certain man was ill, Lazarus of Bethany, the village of
Mary and her sister Martha. Mary was the one who anointed the Lord with perfume and wiped his feet with her hair;
her brother Lazarus was ill. So the sisters sent a message to
Jesus, "Lord, he whom you love is ill." But when Jesus heard
it, he said, "This illness does not lead to death; rather it is for
God's glory.…Accordingly, though Jesus loved Martha and
her sister and Lazarus, after having heard that Lazarus was
ill, he stayed two days longer in the place where he was.

Then after this he said to the disciples, "Let us go to Judea
again."…After saying this, he told them, "Our friend Lazarus
has fallen asleep, but I am going there to awaken him."

When Jesus arrived, he found that Lazarus had already been in the tomb four days....Jesus said to [Martha], "Your brother will rise again." Martha [answered], "I know that he will rise again in the resurrection on the last day." Jesus said to her, "I am the resurrection and the life. Those who believe in me, even though they die, will live, and everyone who lives and believes in me will never die. Do you believe this?" She said to him, "Yes, Lord, I believe that you are the Messiah, the Son of God, the one coming into the world."

When Mary came where Jesus was and saw him, she knelt at his feet and said to him, "Lord, if you had been here, my brother would not have died." When Jesus saw her weeping...he was greatly disturbed in spirit and deeply moved. He said, "Where have you laid him?" They said to him, "Lord, come and see." Jesus began to weep.

Then Jesus, again deeply disturbed, came to the tomb. It was a cave, and a stone was lying against it. Jesus said, "Take away the stone."...So they took away the stone....[H]e cried out with a loud voice, "Lazarus, come out!" The dead man came out, his hands and feet bound with strips of cloth, and his face wrapped in a cloth. Jesus said to them, "Unbind him, and let him go."

RESPONSE   *Seeking God*

Abba Moses asked the Abba Silvanus, "Can a [person] every day make a beginning of the good life?" Abba Silvanus answered him, "If he be diligent, he can every day and every hour begin the good life anew."

ACTION

It is never too late.

God, energy, source of love, bring light out of darkness, order out of chaos, from death creating life. Open our eyes to see, our minds to know, that we may be transformed in Christ, the risen Christ. Amen.

 MIDDAY PRAYER

INVITATION TO PRAYER

O God of strength, come to my assistance. In love for us, you have promised that we can call on your infinite power to give us strength when we have no strength; confidence when all we can see is failure; and hope when ours is gone. We place our lives in your hands, trusting in your promise that in you, all things are possible. Lord, make haste to help me. Amen.

HYMN *Lord of All Hopefulness (v. 2)*

Lord of all eagerness, Lord of all faith,
Whose strong hands were skilled at the plane and the lathe:
Be there at our labors, and give us, we pray,
Your strength in our hearts, Lord, at the noon of the day.

ANTIPHON *2 Corinthians 5:17*

"…if anyone is in Christ, there is a new creation."

PSALM *Psalm 124*

If it had not been the LORD who was on our side
   —let Israel now say—
if it had not been the LORD who was on our side,
   when our enemies attacked us,
then they would have swallowed us up alive,
   when their anger was kindled against us;

then the flood would have swept us away,
   the torrent would have gone over us;
then over us would have gone
   the raging waters.

Blessed be the LORD,
   who has not given us
   as prey to their teeth.
We have escaped like a bird
   from the snare of the fowlers;
   the snare is broken,
   and we have escaped.
Our help is in the name of the LORD,
   who made heaven and earth.

PRAYER TO CARRY WITH ME   *2 Corinthians 5:17*
"…if anyone is in Christ, there is a new creation."

READING   *Isaiah 40:30–31*
Even youths will faint and be weary,
   and the young will fall exhausted;
but those who wait for the LORD shall renew their strength,
   they shall mount up with wings like eagles,
they shall run and not be weary,
   they shall walk and not [be] faint.

RESPONSE
Breathe on me, breath of God,
   fill me with life anew,
that I may love the things you love,
   and do what you would do.

ACTION
It is never too late.

CONCLUDING PRAYER
Loving God, we have not won your favor with our good deeds, beauty, status, wealth, or even by our intentions to do good. When we are ready, you bring your gift of grace and meet us where we are, no matter the chaos or disorder in our lives. You have given each of us gifts and talents uniquely suited to the work you are calling us to do. Help us to use them wisely. Amen.

 EVENING PRAYER

INVITATION TO PRAYER
O Lord of compassion, lift our burdens and let us rejoice in the love that makes us the sheep of your pasture. You are the Good Shepherd who will not rest until you have found us and liberated us from the death-in-life we fall into. Teach us how to choose You, because you are Life. Amen.

HYMN   *Lord of All Hopefulness (v. 3)*
Lord of all kindliness, Lord of all grace,
Your hands swift to welcome, your arms to embrace:
Be there at our homing, and give us, we pray,
Your love in our hearts, Lord, at the eve of the day.

ANTIPHON   *John 10:14*
I know my own and my own know me….

PSALM   *Psalm 23*
The LORD is my shepherd, I shall not want.
   He makes me lie down in green pastures;

he leads me beside still waters;
   he restores my soul.
He leads me in right paths
   for his name's sake.

Even though I walk through the darkest valley,
   I fear no evil;
for you are with me;
   your rod and your staff—
   they comfort me.

You prepare a table before me
   in the presence of my enemies;
you anoint my head with oil;
   my cup overflows.
Surely goodness and mercy shall follow me
   all the days of my life,
and I shall dwell in the house of the LORD
   my whole life long.

PRAYER TO CARRY WITH ME
John 10:14

I know my own and my own know me.

READING
Matthew 18:12–14

What do you think? If a shepherd has a hundred sheep, and one of them has gone astray, does he not leave the ninety-nine on the mountains and go in search of the one that went astray? And if he finds it, truly I tell you, he rejoices over it more than over the ninety-nine that never went astray. So it is not the will of your Father in heaven that one of these little ones should be lost.

RESPONSE

Acts of the Apostles 18:9–10

The Lord said to Paul…"Do not be afraid…for I am with you."

READING

John 10:1–4

"Very truly, I tell you, anyone who does not enter the sheepfold by the gate but climbs in by another way is a thief and a bandit. The one who enters by the gate is the shepherd of the sheep. The gatekeeper opens the gate for him, and the sheep hear his voice. He calls his own sheep by name and leads them out. When he has brought out all his own, he goes ahead of them, and the sheep follow him because they know his voice. "

RESPONSE

Seeking God

[Friends], you will find stability at the moment when you discover that God is everywhere, that you do not need to seek Him elsewhere, that He is here, and if you do not find Him here it is useless to go and search for Him elsewhere because it is not Him that is absent from us, it is we who are absent from Him.

ACTION

It is never too late.

CONCLUDING PRAYER

Lord, you know where I am. You know my struggles and my joys, my strengths and my weaknesses. Temptations are all around me, but what promises relief from my fatigue, my powerlessness, my loneliness and isolation, my failure to live up to my intelligence and opportunities, ends up making it all worse. I've lost my way, Lord; please, come and find me. Amen.

INVITATION TO PRAYER   *The Liturgy of the Hours*

O Lord of calm, today's work is over. Thank you for this moment of rest and reflection. Remind me to step back from my obligations, to inhale your Spirit, and to exhale the worries, disappointments, and frustrations of this day. Cleanse my memory of all that was not good and kind, generous and loving. Help me to clear a space where we can meet, in your peace. Amen.

HYMN   *Lord of All Hopefulness (v. 4)*

Lord of all gentleness, Lord of all calm,
Whose voice is contentment, whose presence is balm:
Be there at our sleeping, and give us, we pray,
Your peace in our hearts, Lord, at the end of the day.

**SILENT REFLECTION ON THE DAY
AND ON OURSELVES**

ANTIPHON   *Psalm 91:2*

[I]…will say to the LORD, "My refuge and my fortress;
    my God in whom I trust."

PSALM   *Psalm 91*

You who live in the shelter of the Most High,
    who abide in the shadow of the Almighty,
will say to the LORD, "My refuge and my fortress;
    my God, in whom I trust."
For he will deliver you from the snare of the fowler
    and from the deadly pestilence;
he will cover you with his pinions,
    and under his wings you will find refuge;
    his faithfulness is a shield and buckler.

You will not fear the terror of the night,
   or the arrow that flies by day,
or the pestilence that stalks in darkness,
   or the destruction that wastes at noonday.

A thousand may fall at your side,
   ten thousand at your right hand,
   but it will not come near you.
You will only look with your eyes
   and see the punishment
   of the wicked.

Because you have made the LORD your refuge,
   the Most High your dwelling place,
no evil shall befall you,
   no scourge come near your tent.

For he will command his angels concerning you
   to guard you in all your ways.
On their hands they will bear you up,
   so that you will not dash your foot against a stone.
You will tread on the lion and the adder,
   the young lion and the serpent
      you will trample under foot.

Those who love me, I will deliver;
   I will protect those who know my name.
When they call to me, I will answer them;
   I will be with them in trouble,
   I will rescue them and honor them.
With long life I will satisfy them,
   and show them my salvation.

PRAYER TO CARRY WITH ME
Psalm 91:2

[I]…will say to the LORD, "My refuge and my fortress;
  my God, in whom I trust."

READING
Luke 1:46–53

And Mary said,
"My soul magnifies the Lord,
  and my spirit rejoices in God my Savior,
for he has looked with favor on the lowliness of his servant.
  Surely, from now on all generations will call me blessed;
for the Mighty One had done great things for me,
  and holy is his name.
His mercy is for those who fear him
  from generation to generation.
He has shown strength with his arm;
  he has scattered the proud in the thoughts of their hearts.
He has brought down the powerful from their thrones,
  and lifted up the lowly;
he has filled the hungry with good things,
  and sent the rich away empty."

Let it be with me as he has said.

RESPONSE
Lord, let me learn to exchange "my will" for "thy will."

SILENT PRAYER FOR THE WORLD, OTHERS, AND OURSELVES

ACTION
I will think and pray about God's promises of abundant life,
to see if I can believe that, in truth, "it is never too late."

Lord, God, send peaceful sleep
  to refresh our tired bodies.
May your help always renew us
  and keep us strong in your service.
We ask this through Christ our Lord. Amen.

STATION 3 ~ *Jesus falls the first time*

ADDICTION ISSUES ~ *Grip of sin, idolatry, obedience*

 MORNING PRAYER

INVITATION TO PRAYER   *Thine the Amen*

O Lord, Holy Spirit, you speak to us in whatever way we have
to listen. In prayer, in music, in silence, in each other, you are
there if we choose to hear you. Let our choice, today, be for *you*
rather than for all the things we think will fill our emptiness,
isolation, and longing. Fill us with your spirit, Lord. Amen.

HYMN   *Lord, Speak to Us, That We May Speak*

Lord, speak to us, that we may speak
In living echoes of your tone;
As you have sought, so let us seek
Your straying children, lost and lone.

Oh, lead us, Lord, that we may lead
The wand'ring and the wav'ring feet;
Oh, feed us, Lord, that we may feed
Your hung'ring ones with manna sweet.

Oh, teach us, Lord, that we may teach
The precious truths which you impart;
And wing our words, that they may reach
The hidden depths of many a heart.

Oh, fill us with your fullness, Lord,
Until our very hearts o'er flow
In kindling thought and glowing word,
Your love to tell, your praise to show.

Psalm 32:7

You are a hiding place for me;
> you preserve me from trouble.

PSALM *Psalm 32:5–7, 8–12*

I acknowledged my sin to you,
> and I did not hide my iniquity;
I said, "I will confess my transgressions to the LORD,"
> and you forgave the guilt of my sin.

Therefore let all who are faithful
> offer prayer to you;
at a time of distress, the rush of mighty waters
> shall not reach them.
You are a hiding place for me;
> you preserve me from trouble....

I will instruct you and teach you the way you should go;
> I will counsel you with my eye upon you.
Do not be like a horse or a mule, without understanding,
> whose temper must be curbed with bit and bridle,
> else it will not stay near you.

Many are the torments of the wicked,
> but steadfast love surrounds those who trust in the LORD.
Be glad in the LORD and rejoice, O righteous,
> and shout for joy, all you upright in heart.

PRAYER TO CARRY WITH ME *Psalm 32:7*

You are a hiding place for me;
> you preserve me from trouble.

READING *Acts of the Apostles 2:1–12*

When the day of Pentecost had come, they [the apostles]

were all together in one place. And suddenly from heaven there came a sound like the rush of a violent wind, and it filled the entire house where they were sitting. Divided tongues, as of fire, appeared among them, and a tongue rested on each of them. All of them were filled with the Holy Spirit and began to speak in other languages, as the Spirit gave them ability.

Now there were devout Jews from every nation under heaven living in Jerusalem. And at this sound the crowd gathered and was bewildered, because each one heard them speaking in the native language of each. Amazed and astonished, they asked, "Are not all these who are speaking Galileans? And how is it that we hear, each of us, in our own native language? Parthians, Medes, Elamites, and residents of Mesopotamia, Judea…and Asia, Egypt…Libya…Cyrene, and visitors from Rome, both Jews and proselytes [visitors from Crete], and Arabs—in our own languages we hear them [the apostles] speaking about God's deeds of power." All were amazed and perplexed, saying to one another, "What does this mean?"

RESPONSE

When God calls, are we listening? Do we listen only with our ears, or with our hearts also? What keeps us from hearing and understanding? We come to know God the Father by his creative power and his laws. We come to know God the Son through his healing, forgiveness, and salvation. How do we come to know God the Holy Spirit, who brings the grace that sustains us in our daily lives?

ACTION

Today, look for signs of the Holy Spirit's presence, the spark that connects us to one another and to God.

Lord, teach us to see thee
    not just in stained glass
    but in stained lives;
    not in Gothic arches,
    but in arthritic fingers.
Lord, teach us to hear thee
    not just in hymns of praise
    but in sneers of distain.
Lord, let us know thee [you] and love thee [you]
    in all things as thou lovest [you love] us—
For thou lovest [you love]
    the self-seeking as well as the unselfish;
    the vindictive as well as the kind,
    the sinners as well as the saints.
Thou lovest [You love] even me, Lord.

THE REVEREND VIRGINIA C. THOMAS

 MIDDAY PRAYER

INVITATION TO PRAYER

O Lord, your strength is above all strength, yet you fell,
and not just once. Help us know the strength that let you fall
to raise us up. Help us trust in your strength when we are
buffeted by desires and longings that promise relief, yet lead
us deeper into darkness. Amen.

HYMN *Thy Strong Word*

Thy strong word did cleave the darkness;
At thy speaking it was done.
For created light we thank thee,
While thine ordered seasons run.

Refrain
Alleluia! Alleluia! Praise to thee who light dost send!
Alleluia! Alleluia! Alleluia! without end!

Lo, on those who dwelt in darkness,
Dark as night and deep as death,
Broke the light of thy salvation,
Breathed thine own life-giving breath.

Refrain

ANTIPHON   *Psalm 5:8*
Lead me, O LORD...
    make your way straight before me.

PSALM   *Psalm 31:9, 14–17, 19–20, 22–24*
Be gracious to me, O LORD, for I am in distress;
    my eye wastes away from grief,
    my soul and body also....

But I trust in you, O LORD;
    I say, "You are my God."
My times are in your hand;
    deliver me from the hand of my enemies and persecutors.
Let your face shine upon your servant;
    save me in your steadfast love.
Do not let me be put to shame, O LORD,
    for I call on you;
let the wicked be put to shame;
    let them go dumbfounded to [the grave]....

O how abundant is your goodness
    that you have laid up for those who fear you,

and accomplished for those who take refuge in you,
  in the sight of everyone!
In the shelter of your presence you hide them
  from human plots;
you hold them safe under your shelter….

I had said in my alarm,
  "I am driven far from your sight."
But you heard my supplications
  when I cried out to you for help.

Love the LORD, all you his saints.
  The LORD preserves the faithful….
Be strong, and let your heart take courage,
  all you who wait for the LORD.

PRAYER TO CARRY WITH ME   *Psalm 5:8*
Lead me, O LORD…
  make your way straight before me.

READING   *Acts of the Apostles 7:58 — 8:1–3;*
                       9:1–7, 8–13, 15–19

Then they dragged [Stephen] out of the city and began to stone
him; and the witnesses laid their coats at the feet of a young
man named Saul.…And Saul approved of their killing him.

  That day a severe persecution began against the church
in Jerusalem.…Saul was ravaging the church by entering
house after house; dragging off both men and women…still
breathing threats and murder against the disciples of the
Lord, [he] went to the high priest and asked him for letters
to the synagogues at Damascus, so that if he found any
who belonged to the Way, men or women, he might bring
them bound to Jerusalem. Now as he was…approaching

Damascus, suddenly a light from heaven flashed around him. He fell to the ground and heard a voice saying to him, "Saul, Saul, why do you persecute me?" He asked, "Who are you, Lord?" The reply came, "I am Jesus, whom you are persecuting. But get up and enter the city, and you will be told what…to do." The men who were traveling with him stood speechless because they heard the voice but saw no one. Saul got up from the ground, and though his eyes were open, he could see nothing; so they led him by the hand and brought him into Damascus. For three days he was without sight, and neither ate nor drank.

Now there was a disciple in Damascus named Ananias. The Lord said to him in a vision, "Ananias." He answered, "Here I am, Lord." The Lord said to him, "Get up and go to the street called Straight, and…look for a man of Tarsus named Saul. At this moment he is praying, and he has seen in a vision a man named Ananias come in and lay his hands on him so that he might regain his sight." But Ananias answered, "Lord, I have heard from many about this man, how much evil he has done to your saints in Jerusalem."….But the Lord said to him, "Go, for he is an instrument whom I have chosen to bring my name before Gentiles…and before the people of Israel; I myself will show him how much he must suffer for the sake of my name." So Ananias went and…laid his hands on Saul and said, "Brother Saul, the Lord Jesus, who appeared to you on your way here, has sent me so that you may regain your sight and be filled with the Holy Spirit." And immediately something like scales fell from his eyes, and his sight was restored. Then he got up and was baptized, and after taking some food, he regained his strength.

RESPONSE   *You Are Mine (David Haas)*

Do not be afraid, I am with you.
I have called you each by name.

Come and follow me, I will bring you home;
I love you and you are mine.

ACTION

Today, look for signs of the Holy Spirit's presence, the spark that connects us to one another and to God.

CONCLUDING PRAYER

Oh God of Love, you give us so much, your faithful presence, our gifts and talents, other people. Remove the scales from our eyes, and from our hearts. Show us how to see ourselves as you see us. Teach us to feel your longing for us, as we long for whatever we think can take your place. Help us to remember, every day, that we never have to settle for second best. Amen.

 EVENING PRAYER

INVITATION TO PRAYER

O Lord, open my lips and my mouth will declare your praise. Cleanse my heart of any worthless, evil, or distracting thoughts. Give me the energy and love to pray with attention, reverence, and devotion. Father, let my prayer be heard in your presence, for it is offered through Christ our Lord. Amen.

HYMN   *"Take Up Your Cross," the Savior Said*

"Take up your cross," the Savior said,
"If you would my disciple be;
Forsake the past, and come this day,
And humbly follow after me."

Take up your cross; let not its weight
Pervade your soul with vain alarm;
His strength shall bear your spirit up,
Sustain your heart, and nerve your arm.

Take up your cross, nor heed the shame,
Nor let your foolish heart rebel;
For you the Lord endured the cross
To save your soul from death and hell.

Take up your cross and follow Christ,
Nor think till death to lay it down;
For only those who bear the cross
May hope to wear a golden crown.

ANTIPHON   *Psalm 25:10*
All the paths of the LORD are steadfast love and faithfulness.

PSALM   *Psalm 25:1–2, 4–10*
To you, O LORD, I lift up my soul.
O my God, in you I trust;
   do not let me be put to shame....

Make me to know your ways, O LORD;
   teach me your paths.
Lead me in your truth, and teach me,
   for you are the God of my salvation;
   for you I wait all day long.

Be mindful of your mercy, O LORD, and of your steadfast love,
for they have been from of old.
Do not remember the sins of my youth or my transgressions;
according to your steadfast love remember me,
for your goodness' sake, O LORD!

Good and upright is the LORD;
therefore he instructs sinners in the way.
He leads the humble in what is right,
and teaches the humble his way.
All the paths of the LORD are steadfast love and faithfulness,
for those who keep his covenant and his decrees.

PRAYER TO CARRY WITH ME
I am not alone.

READING
Matthew 19:16–22
Parable of the Rich Young Man

…someone came to [Jesus] and said, "Teacher, what good
deed must I do to have eternal life?" And he said to him,
"Why do you ask me about what is good? There is only one
who is good. If you wish to enter into life, keep the commandments." He said to him, "Which ones?" And Jesus
said, "You shall not murder; You shall not commit adultery;
You shall not steal; You shall not bear false witness; Honor
your father and mother; also, You shall love your neighbor
as yourself." The young man said to him, "I have kept all of
these; what do I still lack?" Jesus said to him, "If you wish to
be perfect,* go, sell your possessions and give your money to
the poor, and you will have treasure in heaven; then come,
follow me." When the young man heard this word, he went
away grieving, for he had many possessions.

---

*The Greek word is *telios*, meaning whole, or complete.

"No one can serve two masters; for [you] will either hate the one and love the other, or be devoted to the one and despise the other."

ACTION

Today, look for signs of the Holy Spirit's presence,
the spark that connects us to one another and to God.

CONCLUDING PRAYER

When someone steals another's
clothes we call him a thief.
Should we not give the
Same name to one who
Could clothe the naked
And does not?
The bread in your cupboard
Belongs to the hungry;
The coat hanging unused in
Your closet belongs to
The person who needs it;
The shoes rotting in your
Closet belong to the
Person who has no shoes;
The money which you hoard
Up belongs to the poor.

BASIL THE GREAT, BISHOP OF CAESAREA (C. 365)

 NIGHT PRAYER

INVITATION TO PRAYER

Lord, teach us to pray: Our Father, who art in heaven,
hallowed be thy name, thy kingdom come, thy will be

done on earth as it is in heaven. Give us this day our daily bread; and forgive us our trespasses as we forgive those who trespass against us; and lead us not into temptation, but deliver us from evil. For the kingdom, the power, and the glory are yours now and for ever. Amen.

Hymn *Here I Am, Lord (Daniel L. Schutte, SJ)*

I, the Lord of sea and sky, I have heard my people cry.
All who dwell in dark and sin my hand will save.
I, who made the stars of night,
I will make their darkness bright.
Who will bear my light to them? Whom shall I send?

Refrain
Here I am Lord. Is it I, Lord?
  I have heard you calling in the night.
I will go, Lord, if you lead me.
  I will hold your people in my heart.

I, the Lord of snow and rain, I have borne my people's pain.
I have wept for love of them. They turn away.
I will break their hearts of stone,
give them hearts for love alone.
I will speak my word to them. Whom shall I send?

Refrain

I, the Lord of wind and flame, I will tend the poor and lame.
I will set a feast for them. My hand will save.
Finest bread I will provide till their hearts be satisfied.
I will give my life to them. Whom shall I send?

Refrain

ANTIPHON   *Psalm 4:3*

...the LORD hears when I call to him.

PSALM   *Psalm 16:7–11*

I bless the LORD who gives me counsel;
   in the night also my heart instructs me.
I keep the LORD always before me;
   because he is at my right hand, I shall not be moved.

Therefore my heart is glad, and my soul rejoices;
   my body also rests secure.
For you do not give me up to [the grave],
   or let your faithful one see [decay].

You show me the path of life.
   In your presence there is fullness of joy;
   in your right hand are pleasures forevermore.

PRAYER TO CARRY WITH ME   *Psalm 4:3*

...the LORD hears when I call to him.

READING   *1 Samuel 3:1–10, 19*

Now the boy Samuel was ministering to the LORD under Eli.

At that time Eli, whose eyesight had begun to grow dim so that he could not see, was lying down in his room; the lamp of God had not yet gone out, and Samuel was lying down in the temple of the LORD, where the ark of God was. Then the LORD called, "Samuel! Samuel!" and he said, "Here I am!" and ran to Eli, and said, "Here I am, for you called me." But he said, "I did not call; lie down again." So he went and lay down. The LORD called again, "Samuel!" Samuel got up and went to Eli, and said, "Here I am, for you called me." But he said, "I did not call, my son; lie down again." Now Samuel did not yet know the LORD, and the word of the LORD had not yet been revealed to him. The LORD called Samuel again, a third time. And he got up and went to Eli, and said, "Here I am, for you called me." Then Eli perceived that the LORD was calling the boy. Therefore Eli said to Samuel, "Go, lie down; and if he calls you, you shall say, 'Speak, LORD, for your servant is listening.'" So Samuel went and lay down in his place.

Now the LORD came and stood there, calling as before, "Samuel! Samuel!" And Samuel said, "Speak, for your servant is listening."…

As Samuel grew up, the LORD was with him and let none of his words fall to the ground.

RESPONSE
The word of the Lord.
Thanks be to God.

SILENT PRAYER FOR THE WORLD, OTHERS, AND OURSELVES

ACTION
Let me dwell in the Holy Spirit's presence,
in the unquenchable flame of God.

CONCLUDING PRAYER
Lord, in the quiet night, you call us, but we don't hear you;
we turn away. We do not want to hear you. Call me again,
Lord. I will try to listen for your voice. Please, call me again.
Amen.

STATION 4 ~ *Jesus meets his mother*

ADDICTION ISSUES ~ *Unconditional love,*
empathy, compassion

 MORNING PRAYER

INVITATION TO PRAYER

O Lord, open my lips and my mouth will declare your
praise. Give me the patience and generosity to pray with
attention, reverence, and devotion. Let me hear, today, your
feminine voice of wisdom, which is always accessible to me,
and carries your nurturing, unconditional, and everlasting
love. Amen.

HYMN   *Lo, How a Rose Is Growing (v. 2, 4, 5)*

Lo, how a rose [e'er blooming]
    From tender stem hath sprung!
Of Jesse's lineage coming
    As prophets long have sung.
It came a flow'ret bright,
    Amid the cold of winter,
When half-spent was the night.

The rose of which I'm singing,
    Isaiah had foretold.
He came to us through Mary
    Who sheltered him from cold.
Through God's eternal will
    This child to us was given
At midnight calm and still.

This flow'r so small and tender,
    With fragrance fills the air;
His brightness ends the darkness
    That kept the earth in fear.
True God and yet true man,
    He came to save his people
From earth's dark night of sin.

O Savior, child of Mary,
    Who felt all human woe;
O Savior, king of glory,
    Who triumphed o'er our foe:
Bring us at length, we pray,
    To the bright courts of heaven
And into endless day.

ANTIPHON   *Psalm 4:7*
You have put gladness in my heart
    more than when...grain and wine abound.

PSALM   *Psalm 4:1, 3, 7–8*
Answer me when I call, O God of my right!
    You gave me room when I was in distress.
    Be gracious to me, and hear my prayer.

...[remember] that the LORD has set apart
        the faithful for himself;
    the LORD hears when I call to him....

You have put gladness in my heart
    more than when...grain and wine abound.
I will both lie down and sleep in peace;
    for you alone, O LORD, make me lie down in safety.

You have put gladness in my heart
  more than when…grain and wine abound.

READING   *Luke 10:29–37*

…[a man] asked Jesus, "…who is my neighbor?" Jesus
replied, "A man was going down from Jerusalem to Jericho,
and fell into the hands of robbers, who stripped him, beat
him, and went away, leaving him half dead. Now by chance
a priest was going down that road; and when he saw him, he
passed by on the other side. So likewise a Levite, when he
came to the place and saw him, passed by on the other side.
But a Samaritan while traveling came near him; and when
he saw him, he was moved with pity. He went to him and
bandaged his wounds, having poured oil and wine on them.
Then he put him on his own animal, brought him to an inn,
and took care of him.

"The next day he took out two denarii, gave them to the
innkeeper, and said, 'Take care of him; and when I come
back, I will repay you whatever more you spend.' Which of
these three, do you think, was a neighbor to the man who fell
into the hands of robbers?" [The man] said, "The one who
showed him mercy." Jesus said to him, "Go and do likewise."

RESPONSE   *Matthew 25:40*

"Truly I tell you, just as you did it to one of the least of
these…you did it to me."

ACTION

Today, where do I see an opportunity for compassion? The
beggar on the street? An African nation torn apart where
women and children starve and are brutalized? An angry

family member who needs a gentle touch instead of a lecture or a lesson? Within my own criticism of myself?

Today, where do I see an opportunity for compassion?

CONCLUDING PRAYER

Lord, save me from drowning in my wounds, so that I can see what I need to heal, and accept the cleansing and sometimes painful treatment of the "oil of forgiveness" and the "wine of honesty." As I am made whole, and able to be compassionate to myself without guilt, help me to bring your compassion to others through your light that shines in me. Amen.

 MIDDAY PRAYER

INVITATION TO PRAYER

O God of mercy, your space is infinite, and I often get lost in it. Where are you? Near, or far away? I try to remember to draw my strength and perseverance from you, but, as Jesus did on the road to Calvary, I stumble. As you looked to your mother for her love and the consolation of her presence at that terrible time, show me where you are so that I may turn to you for comfort and stay my course. Amen.

HYMN *There's a Wideness in God's Mercy (v. 1–3)*

There's a wideness in God's mercy,
  Like the wideness of the sea;
There's a kindness in his justice
  Which is more than liberty.
There is no place where earth's sorrows
  Are more felt than up in heav'n.
There is no place where earth's failings
  Have such kindly judgment giv'n.

There is welcome for the sinner,
　And a promised grace made good;
There is mercy with the Savior;
　There is healing in his blood.
There is grace enough for thousands
　Of new worlds as great as this;
There is room for fresh creations
　In that upper home of bliss.

For the love of God is broader
　Than the measures of our mind;
And the heart of the eternal
　Is most wonderfully kind.
There is plentiful redemption
　In the blood that has been shed;
There is joy for all the members
　In the sorrows of the head.

ANTIPHON　　　　　　　　　　　　　　*Psalm 34:18*

The LORD is near to the brokenhearted,
　and saves the crushed in spirit.

PSALM　　　　　　　　　　　　　　*Psalm 34:18–22*

The LORD is near to the brokenhearted,
　and saves the crushed in spirit.

Many are the afflictions of the righteous,
　but the LORD rescues them from them all.
He keeps all their bones;
　not one of them will be broken.
Evil brings death to the wicked,
　and those who hate the righteous will be condemned.

The LORD redeems the life of his servants;
   none of those who take refuge in him will be condemned.

PRAYER TO CARRY WITH ME   *Psalm 34:18*

The LORD is near to the brokenhearted,
   and saves the crushed in spirit.

READING   *Matthew 15:22–28*

Just then a Canaanite woman…came out and started shouting, "Have mercy on me, Lord, Son of David, my daughter
is tormented by a demon." But he did not answer her at all.
And his disciples came and urged him, saying, "Send her
away, for she keeps shouting after us." He answered, "I was
sent only to the lost sheep of the house of Israel." But she
came and knelt before him, saying, "Lord, help me." He
answered, "It is not fair to take the children's food and throw
it to the dogs." She said, "Yes, Lord, yet even the dogs eat
the crumbs that fall from their masters' table." Then Jesus
answered her, "Woman, great is your faith! Let it be done for
you as you wish." And her daughter was healed instantly.

RESPONSE

If I follow Jesus' example and am merciful to others, why is
it so hard to have mercy on myself? Because I don't deserve
it? Because I don't know what I *genuinely* need, and am
afraid to find out? Am I living off emotional "crumbs"?

ACTION

Today, where do I see an opportunity for mercy? Overlook-
ing a coworker's embarrassing blunder? Offering to help
an overwhelmed mother with a screaming, overtired child
instead of screaming myself? Canceling a debt owed to me?
   Today, where do I see an opportunity for mercy?

CONCLUDING PRAYER   *Looking at Stars*

The God of curved space,
    the dry God,
is not going to help us,
    but the son,
whose blood spattered the
    hem of his mother's robe.

JANE KENYON

 ## EVENING PRAYER

INVITATION TO PRAYER

O Lord of comfort and safety, not all of us will *become*
mothers, but we have each *had* a mother, whether we knew
her or not. Some of us had complete mothers, some had
none; some mothers were caring and compassionate;
some lost to drugs, or alcohol. Can I ever fill the emptiness
where the unfailing love and security of a mother should be?
Maybe I need to stop trying to fill the hole. Can you help me
turn away from my loss and move toward the only love,
your love, that will never betray me? Amen.

HYMN   *Canticle of Mary*

My soul proclaims the greatness of the Lord;
    my spirit rejoices in God my Savior,
    for he has looked with favor on his lowly servant.
    From this day all generations will call me blessed.
    The Almighty has done great things for me,
    and holy is his name.

He has mercy on those who fear him in every generation.
    He has shown the strength of his arm;
    he has scattered the proud in their conceit.

He has cast down the mighty from their thrones,
    and has lifted up the lowly.
He has filled the hungry with good things,
    and the rich he has sent away empty.

He has come to the help of his servant Israel,
    for he has remembered his promise of mercy,
the promise he made to our fathers,
    to Abraham and his children forever.

Glory to the Father, and to the Son, and to the Holy Spirit;
    as it was in the beginning is now and will be forever.
    Amen.

ANTIPHON *Psalm 25:20*

O guard my life, and deliver me...
    for I take refuge in you.

PSALM *Psalm 25:16–21*

Turn to me and be gracious to me,
    for I am lonely and afflicted.
Relieve the troubles of my heart,
    and bring me out of my distress.
Consider my affliction and my trouble,
    and forgive all my sins.

Consider how many are my foes,
    and with what violent hatred they hate me.
O guard my life, and deliver me; do not let me
    be put to shame, for I take refuge in you.
May integrity and uprightness preserve me,
    for I wait for you.

O guard my life, and deliver me...
> for I take refuge in you.

READING *Luke 1:26–35, 38*

In the sixth month the angel Gabriel was sent by God to a town in Galilee called Nazareth, to a virgin engaged to a man whose name was Joseph, of the house of David. The virgin's name was Mary. And he came to her and said, "Greetings, favored one! The Lord is with you." But she was much perplexed by his words and pondered what sort of greeting this might be. The angel said to her, "Do not be afraid, Mary, for you have found favor with God. And now, you will conceive in your womb and bear a son, and you will name him Jesus. He will be great, and will be called the Son of the Most High, and the Lord God will give to him the throne of his ancestor David. He will reign over the house of Jacob forever, and of his kingdom there will be no end." Mary said to the angel, "How can this be, since I am a virgin?" The angel said to her, "The Holy Spirit will come upon you, and the power of the Most High will overshadow you; therefore the child to be born will be holy; he will be called Son of God."...Then Mary said, "Here am I, the servant of the Lord; let it be with me according to your word."

RESPONSE *Adapted from a homily on Luke 1:46–56 by David Heim*

Mary was able to hold in her heart God's past faithfulness and his promise of salvation and redemption. It gave her courage to accept her own role in God's ultimate purpose to "lift up the lowly" and "fill the hungry with good things"; to proclaim the reign of justice and mercy. She could not have imagined the suffering that would be necessary to bring this about.

Evil, disease, addiction, and death are fierce and tenacious enemies. We wonder, "Will victory *ever* come?" Mary must have wondered that. She sang her song of praise long before God's plan to save us from the grip of sin unfolded in the crowded streets of Jerusalem on the way to the crucifixion; before she watched her beloved son nailed to a cross, where she remained with him until his life blood drained out and soaked the ground she stood on. She must have wondered how she could have been so deluded, to think that God's purposes were about to be fulfilled.

But Mary was not deluded. Her trust in God overrode *everything* else; her faith remained steady. In the middle of our most ferocious battles with addiction, she shows us how to do it even when we don't understand. That is why we can return, again and again, to sing Mary's song; to fit ourselves into God's amazing plan so that when it comes to playing our part, we can, like Mary, say "Yes."

ACTION
Today, I will think deeply about the gifts and talents I have been given, and about what my own part might be in God's work in the world.

CONCLUDING PRAYER   *Mother Teresa*
"Prayer makes your heart bigger, until it is capable
  of containing the gift of God himself."

Jesus, help me to spread your fragrance wherever I am.
Fill my heart with your Spirit and your life.
  Penetrate my being and take such hold of me that
  my life…[radiates] your own life.

Give your light through me and remain…in such a way
    that every soul I come in contact with can feel
    your presence in me.
May people not see me, but see you in me.

Remain in me, so that I shine with your light.…
All light will come from you, Oh Jesus.…You will illuminate
    others through me.…

Place on my lips your greatest praise.…
    May I preach you with actions more than with words,
    with the example of my actions, with the
visible light of the love that comes from you to my heart.
    Amen.

 NIGHT PRAYER

INVITATION TO PRAYER

O God of rest, slow my mind, quiet my thoughts, and bring
me to that still place where you and I shall meet. Help me let
go of today's worries and tomorrow's obligations, as well as
the constant struggle to stay on the path to you. Strip away
the entanglements of the world, and at least for tonight,
let me float in your peace. Amen.

HYMN   Nunc Dimittis *(Simeon's Song)*

Lord, now let your servant go in peace;
    your word has been fulfilled.
My own eyes have seen the salvation
    which you have prepared
    in the sight of ev'-ry people:
A light to reveal you to the nations and
    the glory of your people Israel.

Glory to the Father, and to the Son, and to
the Holy Spirit, as it was in the beginning,
is now, and will be forever. Amen.

SILENT REFLECTION ON THE DAY
AND ON OURSELVES

ANTIPHON   *Psalm 17:8*

Guard me as the apple of [your] eye;
hide me in the shadow of your wings.

PSALM   *Psalm 17:6, 8–15*

I call upon you, for you will answer me, O God;
incline your ear to me, hear my words....

Guard me as the apple of [your] eye;
hide me in the shadow of your wings,
from the wicked who despoil me,
my deadly enemies who surround me.
They close their hearts to pity;
with their mouths they speak arrogantly.
They track me down; now they surround me;
they set their eyes to case me to the ground.
They are like the lion eager to tear,
like a young lion lurking in ambush.

Rise up, O LORD, confront them, overthrow them!
By your sword deliver my life from the wicked,
from mortals—by your hand, O LORD—
from mortals, whose portion in life is in this world.
May their bellies be filled
with what you have stored up for them;
may their children have more than enough;
may they leave something over to their little ones.

As for me, I shall behold your face in righteousness;
   when I awake I shall be satisfied, beholding your likeness.

PRAYER TO CARRY WITH ME
Psalm 17:8

Guard me as the apple of [your] eye;
   hide me in the shadow of your wings.

READING
Luke 2:25–28, 33–35

Now there was a man in Jerusalem whose name was Simeon;
this man was righteous and devout, looking forward to the
consolation of Israel, and the Holy Spirit rested on him. It
had been revealed to him by the Holy Spirit that he would
not see death before he has seen the Lord's Messiah. Guided
by the Spirit, Simeon came into the temple; and when the
parents brought in the child Jesus, to do for him what was
customary under the law, Simeon took him in his arms and
praised God....

   And the child's father and mother were amazed at what
was being said about him. Then Simeon blessed them and
said to his mother Mary, "This child is destined for the
falling and the rising of many in Israel, and to be a sign that
will be opposed so that the inner thoughts of many will be
revealed—and a sword will pierce your own soul too."

RESPONSE
Hebrews 4:15–16

...we have [a Savior] who in every respect has been tested
as we are, yet without sin. Let us...approach the throne of
grace with boldness, so that we may receive mercy and find
grace to help in time of need.

SILENT PRAYER FOR THE WORLD, OTHERS, AND OURSELVES

ACTION

Mary heard Simeon say, "…and a sword will pierce your own soul too." As she held Jesus in her arms she could not have imagined the pain to which she had committed herself. And yet she continued to say "Yes." How can I use my own pain to contribute to the unfolding of God's work within myself and in the world?

CONCLUDING PRAYER

Lord, God, send peaceful sleep
to refresh my body and renew my soul.
Hold and comfort me with your presence
    and your feminine voice of wisdom,
which is always accessible to me, and carries your
    nurturing, unconditional, and everlasting love. Amen.

STATION 5 ~ *Simon helps carry the cross*

ADDICTION ISSUES ~ *Dependence, interdependence, asking for help*

 MORNING PRAYER

INVITATION TO PRAYER

O Jesus, every day I begin anew. I struggle to balance needs and wants, work with rest, other people and solitude, my responsibilities with those that are not mine. I try, but by the end of the day I feel empty and exhausted. I don't know how to refresh myself in healthy ways that give life, not take it away. So, I keep filling the hole as best I can, but I fill it with the wrong things. I can't digest those things anymore, Lord, and they are killing me. Help me to choose life. Amen.

HYMN   *Gift of Finest Wheat*

Refrain
You satisfy the Hungry Heart with gift of finest wheat.
Come give to us, O saving Lord, the bread of life to eat.

As when the shepherd calls his sheep,
    they know and heed his voice;
so when you call your fam-ily Lord,
    we follow and rejoice.

Refrain

Is not the cup we bless and share
    the blood of Christ outpoured?
Do not one cup, one loaf, declare
    our oneness in the Lord?

Refrain

You give yourself to us, O Lord;
  then selfless let us be,
to serve each other in your name
  in truth and charity.

Refrain

ANTIPHON   *Psalm 30:2*
O LORD my God, I cried to you for help,
  and you have healed me.

PSALM   *Psalm 30:1–5*
I will extol you, O LORD, for you have drawn me up,
  and did not let my foes* rejoice over me.
O LORD, my God, I cried to you for help,
  and you have healed me.
O LORD, you brought up my soul from [the dead],
  restored me to life from among
    those gone down to the Pit.

Sing praises to the LORD, O you his faithful ones,
  and give thanks to his holy name.
For his anger is but for a moment;
  his favor is for a lifetime.
Weeping may linger for the night,
  but joy comes with the morning.

---

*Addictive substances and behaviors.

PRAYER TO CARRY WITH ME

O God, I'm dying of hunger and thirst down here and can't seem to find my way out. Rescue me, Lord.

READING

John 21:3–12

Simon Peter said to them [disciples], "I am going fishing." They said to him, "We will go with you." They went out and got into the boat, but that night they caught nothing.

Just after daybreak, Jesus stood on the beach; but the disciples did not know that it was Jesus. Jesus said to them "Children, you have no fish, have you?" They answered him, "No." He said to them, "Cast the net to the right side of the boat, and you will find some." So they cast it, and now they were not able to haul it in because there were so many fish. The disciple whom Jesus loved said to Peter. "It is the Lord!"… [T]he other disciples came in the boat, dragging the net full of fish, for they were not far from the land.…

When they had gone ashore, they saw a charcoal fire there, with fish on it, and bread. Jesus said to them, "Bring some of the fish that you have just caught." So Simon Peter went aboard and hauled the net ashore, full of large fish, a hundred fifty-three of them, and though there were so many, the net was not torn. Jesus said to them, "Come and have breakfast."

RESPONSE

How can we use the model of Jesus' hospitality to learn how to be hospitable to ourselves?

ACTION

Today, Lord, in my prayers, I will not use words or ask for anything. I will wait quietly and watch for you, to hear what you have to say to me. Please let me recognize you; please come to me in a way I can understand.

CONCLUDING PRAYER

Lord Jesus, you fed five thousand people with five barley loaves and two fish, and you fed your disciples on the beach. You showed us we don't need to be afraid that there won't be "enough." You are the Bread of Life. Teach me about what is "enough." Amen.

 MIDDAY PRAYER

INVITATION TO PRAYER

O Lord of generosity, you have promised to give us whatever we ask for, but sometimes it seems as if our asking is not answered. Why is that? I wait and wait for your voice, but I can't hear it. Is it because I'm not asking the right questions?

Is the problem in what I am asking for, or how I am asking for it, or am I looking and listening for the answer in the wrong places? Teach me, Lord, to ask for the right things, the things you would want me to ask for. Show me how to grow from wanting "things" and people to wanting only you. You are the only thing that can fill me up. Amen.

HYMN   *I Received the Living God*
Refrain
I received the living God, and my heart is full of joy,
I received the living God, and my heart is full of joy.

Jesus said: I am the bread kneaded long to give you life;
   you who will partake of me need not ever fear to die.

Refrain

Jesus said: I am the way, and my Father longs for you;
   so I come to bring you home to be one with us anew.

Refrain

Jesus said: I am the truth; if you follow close to me,
   you will know me in your heart, and my word shall make
   you free.

Refrain

Jesus said: I am the life far from whom no thing can grow,
   But receive this living bread, and my Spirit you shall know.

ANTIPHON   *Psalm 3:4*

I cry aloud to the LORD, and he answers me....

PSALM   *Psalm 3*

O LORD, how many are my foes!
   Many are rising against me;
many are saying to me,
   "There is no help for you in God."

But you, O LORD, are a shield around me,
   my glory, and the one who lifts up my head.
I cry aloud to the LORD,
   and he answers me from his holy hill.

I lie down and sleep;
   I wake again for the LORD sustains me.
I am not afraid of ten thousands of people
   who have set themselves against me all around.

Rise up, O LORD!
Deliver me, O my God!
For you strike all my enemies on the cheek;
you break the teeth of the wicked.

Deliverance belongs to the Lord;
may your blessing be on your people!

PRAYER TO CARRY WITH ME

LORD, I shall follow close to thee,
and your word will make me free.

READING
John 6:3, 5, 7–13

Jesus went up the mountain and sat down there with his
disciples.…When he looked up and saw a large crowd
coming toward him, Jesus said to Philip, "Where are we to
buy bread for these people to eat?"…Philip answered him,
"Six months' wages would not buy enough bread for each
of them to get a little." One of his disciples, Andrew, Simon
Peter's brother, said to him, "There is a boy here who has five
barley loaves and two fish. But what are they among so many
people?" Jesus said, "Make the people sit down."…[S]o
they sat down, about five thousand in all. Then Jesus took
the loaves, and when he had given thanks, he distributed
them to those who were seated; so also the fish, as much as
they wanted. When they were satisfied, he told his disciples,
"Gather up the fragments left over, so that nothing may be
lost." So they gathered them up, and from the fragments of
the five barley loaves, left by those who had eaten, they filled
twelve baskets.

RESPONSE
"Just enough is plenty."

BARBARA DIAMOND GOLDIN

ACTION
Today, Lord, in my prayers, I will not use words or ask for anything. I will wait quietly and watch for you, to hear what you have to say to me. Please let me recognize you; please come to me in a way I can understand.

CONCLUDING PRAYER
Lord Jesus, you fed five thousand people with five barley loaves and two fish, and you fed your disciples on the beach. You showed us we need not be afraid that there won't be "enough." You are the Bread of Life. Teach me what is "enough." Amen.

 EVENING PRAYER

INVITATION TO PRAYER
O God of grace, today you have shown me how foolish it is to think I can carry my burdens, do my work, and find my way alone. When responsibilities feel too great, instead of turning to you, my only true help, I use tricksters to ease my anxiety, numb the chafing of the yoke on my neck, and send me in what seems a good direction but is really a dead end. At the close of this workday, give me true rest and refreshment. Help me to learn the difference between authentic hunger and heart hunger, to resist the temptation to substitute real satisfaction from the "quick fix" phony that beckons me when I feel empty. Renew my strength and energy, Lord. Amen.

Eternal Father, strong to save,
Whose arm has bound the restless wave,
Who bade the mighty ocean deep
Its own appointed limits keep:
Oh, hear us when we cry to thee
For those in peril on the sea.

O Savior, whose almighty word
The winds and waves submissive heard,
Who walked upon the foaming deep,
And calm amid the storm didst sleep:
Oh, hear us when we cry to thee
For those in peril on the sea.

O Holy Spirit, who didst brood
Upon the chaos dark and rude,
And bid its angry tumult cease,
And give, for wild confusion, peace:
Oh, hear us when we cry to thee
For those in peril on the sea.

ANTIPHON   *Psalm 1:1–3*

Happy are those…
    [whose] delight is in the Lord.…
In all that they do, they prosper.

PSALM   *Psalm 1:1–3*

Happy are those…
    [whose] delight is in the LORD.…
They are like trees
    planted by streams of water,

which yield their fruit in its season,
   and their leaves do not wither.
In all that they do, they prosper.

PRAYER TO CARRY WITH ME

Lord, Peter's faith gave him the courage to walk toward you
across the water, but he faltered when his focus on you faltered. Strengthen me in my faith, and help me to remember
that faithful courage is "to be afraid and do it anyway."

READING   *Matthew 14:22–33*

Immediately [after feeding the five thousand, Jesus] made
the disciples get into the boat and go on ahead to the other
side, while he dismissed the crowds. And after he had dismissed the crowds, he went up the mountain by himself to
pray. When evening came, he was there alone, but by this
time the boat, battered by the waves, was far from the land,
for the wind was against them. And early in the morning he
came walking toward them on the sea. But when the disciples saw him walking on the sea, they were terrified, saying,
"It's a ghost!" And they cried out in fear. But immediately
Jesus spoke to them and said, "Take heart, it is I; do not be
afraid."

Peter answered him, "Lord, if it is you, command me to
come to you on the water." He said, "Come." So Peter got out
of the boat, started walking on the water, and came toward
Jesus. But when he noticed the strong wind, he became
frightened, and beginning to sink, he cried out, "Lord, save
me!" Jesus immediately reached his hand and caught him,
saying to him, "You of little faith, why did you doubt?" When
they got into the boat, the wind ceased. And those in the boat
worshiped him, saying, "Truly you are the Son of God."

A True Story (from Maximum *Security)*

There was a man wrongfully convicted of a terrible crime, the rape and murder of a nurse who lived nearby, and he was sentenced to forty years in prison. He and his wife and little children were separated because he was moved to a maximum security facility in another part of the state. Their strong faith supported them through the injustice of this conviction and the brutality of prison life, but with the realization that even if the verdict were to be reversed by some miracle, he particularly, and their young family in general, would be stigmatized for life.

After seven years, with the help of a *pro bono* lawyer, and the development of DNA testing, he was exonerated, conclusively. When his father-in-law spoke at the community celebration, following his release, he gave powerful witness to how this young family had been sustained through their ordeal. "The answer is not in *what*, but in *whom*, and it comes in the image of Peter walking on the water toward Christ. Keeping his eye on Christ, he would not sink. Today is a celebration of that faith."

ACTION

Today, Lord, in my prayers, I will not use words or ask for anything. I will wait quietly and watch for you, to hear what you have to say to me. Please let me recognize you; please come to me in a way I can understand.

CONCLUDING PRAYER

Lord Jesus, you fed five thousand people with barely enough food to feed five. You walked on water and called Peter, in faith, to walk to you. You surprised your disciples with a bounteous catch of fish, and then invited them to breakfast with you on the beach. Surprise me, Lord. Come to me in my ordinary, everyday life. Surprise me. Amen.

 NIGHT PRAYER

INVITATION TO PRAYER
The end of the day, Lord. I did my best, but somehow it doesn't feel that way.

I look forward to this time with you; I'm alone, it's quiet, no one will ask me to do one more task. But I am beset with worry about things left undone, things I should have done better, someone I might have offended. Teach me to replace "should" with "is"; to "describe," not "evaluate." To accept myself with all my flaws and failures and learn to see myself as you do. Help me die to this anxiety and bring to life a sacred space where we can meet. Amen.

HYMN   *Lamb of God*
Lamb of God, you take away the sins of the world:
    have mercy on us,

Lamb of God, you take away the sins of the world:
    have mercy on us.

Lamb of God, you take away the sins of the world:
    grant us peace.

**SILENT REFLECTION ON THE DAY
AND ON OURSELVES**

ANTIPHON   *Philippians 4:13*
I can do all things through him who strengthens me.

PSALM   *Psalm 25:1, 4–5, 8, 10, 11–12, 15, 21*

To you, O LORD, I lift up my soul.…

Make me to know your ways, O LORD;
    teach me your paths.
Lead me in your truth, and teach me,
    for you are the God of my salvation;
    for you I wait all day long.…

Good and upright is the LORD;
    therefore he instructs sinners in the way.…
All the paths of the LORD are
    steadfast love and faithfulness.…

For your name's sake, O LORD,
    pardon my guilt, for it is great.
Who are they that fear the LORD?
    He will teach them the way that they should choose.…

My eyes are ever toward the LORD,
    for he will pluck my feet out of the net.…

May integrity and uprightness preserve me,
    for I wait for you.

PRAYER TO CARRY WITH ME   *Philippians 4:13*

I can do all things through him who strengthens me.

READING   *Luke 5:17–20, 24, 25*

One day, while [Jesus] was teaching, Pharisees and teachers
of the law were sitting near by…and the power of the Lord
was with him to heal. Just then some men came, carrying a
paralyzed man on a bed. They were trying to bring him in
and lay him before Jesus; but finding no way to bring him in

because of the crowd, they went up on the roof and let him down with his bed through [an opening in] the tiles into the middle of the crowd in front of Jesus. When [Jesus] saw their faith, he said, "Friend, your sins are forgiven you."…"I say to you, stand up and take your bed and go to your home."

RESPONSE

Do I have friends who would stop at nothing to bring me to a healing place?

Am I that kind of friend? To myself?

SILENT PRAYER FOR THE WORLD, OTHERS, AND OURSELVES

Our Father

Our Father, who art in heaven, hallowed be thy name;
thy kingdom come, thy will be done on earth as it is in
heaven.
Give us this day our daily bread; and forgive us our
trespasses, as we forgive those who trespass against us;
and lead us not into temptation, but deliver us from evil.
For the kingdom, the power, and the glory are yours
now and for ever. Amen.

ACTION

Tonight, Lord, in my prayers, I will not use words or ask for anything.

I will wait quietly and listen for you in the darkness.
I have opened my heart to make a sacred space; please come to me there.

Protect us, Lord, as we stay awake;
    watch over us as we sleep,
that awake, we may keep watch
    with Christ,
        and asleep, rest in his peace. Amen.

STATION 6 ~ *Veronica wipes the face of Jesus*

ADDICTION ISSUES ~ *Confession, abundance, gratitude*

 MORNING PRAYER

INVITATION TO PRAYER

O generous God, today I will accept your invitation to become an active part of your creativity in the world. It seems selfish to focus on what *I want*. Could you show me how to have and do what *you want?* Where will that lead me? I am already too busy to add any new "creative" activities. Maybe I will have to watch some of my current life slide off and away. Do I have to give up *everything* to belong to you? I will ask. Amen.

HYMN   **Ubi Caritas et Amor** *(Taizé)*

Ubi caritas et amor
Where true charity and love abide
Ubi caritas Deus ibi est.
God is dwelling there; God is dwelling there.

ANTIPHON   *Psalm 34:10*

...[T]hose who seek the LORD lack no good thing.

PSALM   *Psalm 34:1–22*

I will bless the LORD at all times;
   his praise shall continually be in my mouth....
   let the humble hear and be glad.
O magnify the LORD with me,
   and let us exalt his name together.

I sought the LORD, and he answered me,
and delivered me from all my fears.
Look to him, and be radiant;
so your faces shall never be ashamed.
This poor soul cried, and was heard by the LORD,
and was saved from every trouble.
The angel of the LORD encamps
around those who fear him, and delivers them.
O taste and see that the LORD is good;
happy are those who take refuge in him.…
The young lions suffer want and hunger,
but those who seek the LORD lack no good thing.

Come, O children, listen to me;
I will teach you the fear of the LORD.
Which of you desires life,
and covets many days to enjoy good?
Keep your tongue from evil,
and your lips from speaking deceit.
Depart from evil, and do good;
seek peace, and pursue it.

The eyes of the LORD are on the righteous,
and his ears are open to their cry.…
When the righteous cry for help, the LORD hears,
and rescues them from all their troubles.
The LORD is near to the brokenhearted,
and saves the crushed in spirit.

Many are the afflictions of the righteous,
but the LORD rescues them from them all.
He keeps all their bones;
not one of them will be broken.…

The LORD redeems the life of his servants;
none of those who take refuge in him will be condemned.

PRAYER TO CARRY WITH ME

Psalm 34:10

…[T]hose who seek the LORD lack no good thing.

READING

Luke 11:9–13

"So I say to you, Ask, and it will be given you; search, and
you will find; knock, and the door will be opened for you.
For everyone who asks receives, and everyone who searches
finds, and for everyone who knocks, the door will be opened.
Is there anyone among you who, if your child asks for a fish,
will give a snake instead of a fish? Or if the child asks for an
egg, will give a scorpion? If you then, who are evil, know
how to give good gifts to your children, how much more will
the heavenly Father give the Holy Spirit to those who ask
him!"

RESPONSE

Matthew 7:12

"In everything, do to others as you would have them
do to you.…"

ACTION

Today I will make a choice to seek one small area of my life
where I will "turn" and ask God to help me heal.

CONCLUDING PRAYER

Our Father, who art in heaven,
Are you really there, Lord?
hallowed be thy name.
Am I clean and straight enough to be with you?
Thy kingdom come,
*Is this when there will be no more pain, disappointment,
cruelty, addiction?*

thy will be done on earth as it is in heaven.

Because your will can be *our will?*

Give us this day our daily bread;

How much do we get? It never feels like enough.

and forgive us our trespasses,

Where to begin?

as we forgive those who trespass against us;

Sometimes I don't want to forgive their sins.

and lead us not into temptation,

I lead myself there; it's everywhere.

but deliver us from evil.

The evil I do to others, the evil they do to me,
and the evil I do to myself.

For the kingdom, the power, and the glory are yours

I'm really not *responsible for everything.*

now and for ever. Amen.

Amen.

 MIDDAY PRAYER

INVITATION TO PRAYER

Merciful Lord, it takes only a moment for us to find ourselves in the midst of trouble others have lived with without
hope of relief. Our health is destroyed, a loved one is lost,
a natural disaster explodes a life that will never be the same.
It is tempting to reach for something that will drown our
pain, obliterate our loss. Help us remember to call on you,
as the only true comfort, with confidence you are always
with us. Amen.

Lord Jesus from your wounded side
   flowed streams of cleansing water,
   alleluia, alleluia, alleluia.
The world was washed of all its sin
   all life made new again,
   alleluia, alleluia, alleluia.

Repeat

ANTIPHON   *Psalm 28:6*

Blessed be the LORD,
   for he has heard the sound of my pleadings.

PSALM   *Psalm 28:6–9*

Blessed be the LORD,
   for he has heard the sound of my pleadings.
The LORD is my strength and my shield;
   in him my heart trusts;
so I am helped, and my heart exults,
   and with my song I give thanks to him.

The LORD is the strength of his people
   he is the saving refuge of his anointed.
O save your people, and bless your heritage;
   be their shepherd, and carry them forever.

PRAYER TO CARRY WITH ME   *Psalm 28:6*

Blessed be the LORD,
   for he has heard the sound of my pleadings.

READING   *John 5:2–9*

Now in Jerusalem by the Sheep Gate there is a pool, called
in Hebrew Beth-zatha, which has five porticoes. In these lay

many invalids—blind, lame, and paralyzed. One man was there who had been ill for thirty-eight years. When Jesus saw him lying there and knew that he had been there a long time, he said to him, "Do you want to be made well?" The sick man answered him, "Sir, I have no one to put me into the pool when the water is stirred up; and while I am making my way, someone else steps down ahead of me." Jesus said to him, "Stand up, take your mat and walk." At once the man was made well, and he took up his mat and began to walk.

RESPONSE   *Isaiah 43:1, 2, 4*

But now thus says the LORD…
> he who created you…
> he who formed you.…
Do not fear, for I have redeemed you;
> I have called you by name, you are mine.
When you pass through the waters, I will be with you;
> and through the rivers, they shall not overwhelm you;
when you walk through fire you shall not be burned,
> and the flame shall not consume you.…
Because you are precious in my sight,
> and honored, and I love you.

ACTION
Today, I will make a choice to seek one small area of my life where I will "turn" and ask God to help me heal.

CONCLUDING PRAYER
Gentle God, you remind me that you are my faithful friend, and that you will deliver me from the chains that keep me from the fullness of life. I bless you for this in love and in confidence in Jesus' name. Amen.

INVITATION TO PRAYER

Generous God, you are ready to give me my heart's desire,
if only I will ask, in confidence, and receive, with faith in
your love. Help me to align *my* will with *thy* will, so what
I fervently seek is exactly what you know I need, and want
me to have. Amen.

HYMN   *Eye Has Not Seen (Marty Haugen)*

Refrain
Eye has not seen, ear has not heard what God has ready
  for those who love him;
Spirit of love, come, give us the mind of Jesus, teach us the
  wisdom of God.

When pain and sorrow weigh us down, be near to us,
    O Lord,
forgive the weakness of our faith, and bear us up
    within your peaceful word.

Refrain

Our lives are but a single breath, we flower and we fade,
yet all our days are in your hands, so we return in love
    what love has made.

Refrain

To those who see with eyes of faith, the Lord is ever near,
reflected in the faces, of all the poor and lowly of the world.

Refrain

We sing a mys-t'ry from the past in halls
   where saints have trod,
yet ever new the music rings to Jesus, Living Song of God.

Refrain

ANTIPHON   *Psalm 119:10*
With my whole heart I seek you....

PSALM   *Psalm 119:10–12, 15*
With my whole heart I seek you;
   do not let me stray from your commandments.
I treasure your word in my heart,
   so that I may not sin against you.
Blessed are you, O LORD;
   teach me your statutes....
I will meditate on your precepts,
   and fix my eyes on your ways.

PRAYER TO CARRY WITH ME   *Psalm 119:10*
With my whole heart I seek you....

READING   *John 9:1–12*
As he walked along, [Jesus] saw a man blind from birth. His
disciples asked him, "Rabbi, who sinned, this man or his
parents, that he was born blind?" Jesus answered, "Neither
this man nor his parents sinned; he was born blind so that
God's works might be revealed in him. We must work the
works of him who sent me while it is day; night is coming
when no one can work. As long as I am in the world, I am
the light of the world." When he had said this, he spat on
the ground and made mud with the saliva and spread the
mud on the man's eyes, saying to him, "Go, wash in the pool
of Siloam" (which means Sent). Then he went and washed

and came back able to see. The neighbors and those who had seen him before as a beggar began to ask, "Is this not the man who used to sit and beg?" Some were saying, "It is he." Others were saying, "No, but it is someone like him." He kept saying, "I am the man." But they kept asking him, "Then how were your eyes opened?" He answered, "The man called Jesus made mud, spread it on my eyes, and said to me, 'Go to Siloam and wash.' Then I went and washed and received my sight." They said to him, "Where is he?" He said, "I do not know."

RESPONSE   *John 12:37, 38, 40*
After Jesus had said this, he departed and hid from them. Although he had performed so many signs in their presence, they did not believe in him. This was to fulfill the word spoken by the prophet Isaiah:

"He has blinded their eyes
    and hardened their heart,
so that they might not look with their eyes,
    and understand with their heart and turn—
        and I would heal them."

ACTION
Today, I will make a choice to seek one small area of my life where I can "turn" and ask God to help me heal.

CONCLUDING PRAYER
Breathe on me, breath of God,
fill me with life anew,
that I may love the things you love,
and do what you would do.
Amen.

O God of quiet, calm my heart, slow my pace, and help me
to gently disengage from all the things this day has brought.
Turn my soul toward your rhythms and delights, where I
can enjoy my successes and ask forgiveness for my failures.
Help me to see when my will was aligned with your will, and
give me the energy for tomorrow, not knowing what it will
bring, but sensing your love and support beneath me. Amen.

HYMN *Psalmody for Evening Prayer (Vespers)*
Let my prayer rise before you as incense;
the lifting up of my hands as the evening sacrifice.

O Lord, I call to you; come to me quickly;
hear my voice when I cry to you.

Let my prayer rise before you as incense;
the lifting up of my hands as the evening sacrifice.

Set a watch before my mouth, O Lord,
and guard the door of my lips.

Let not my heart incline to any evil thing;
let me not be occupied in wickedness with evildoers.

But my eyes are turned to you, Lord God;
in you I take refuge. Strip me not of my life.

Glory to the Father, and to the Son, and to the Holy Spirit;
as it was in the beginning, is now, and will be forever. Amen.

Let my prayer rise before you as incense;
the lifting up of my hands as the evening sacrifice.

SILENT REFLECTION ON THE DAY
AND ON OURSELVES

ANTIPHON *Psalm 40:6*

...you have given me an open ear.

PSALM *Psalm 40:1, 3–4, 6–8, 10–11*

I waited patiently for the LORD;
   he inclined to me and heard my cry....
He put a new song in my mouth,
   a song of praise to our God.
Many will see and fear,
   and put their trust in the LORD.

Happy are those who make
   the LORD their trust,
who do not turn to the proud,
   to those who go astray after false gods....

Sacrifice and offering you do not desire,
   but you have given me an open ear....
Then I said, "Here I am;
   in the scroll of the book it is written of me.
I delight to do your will, O my God;
   your law is within my heart."...

I have not hidden your saving help within my heart,
   I have spoken of your faithfulness and your salvation;
I have not concealed your steadfast love
   and your faithfulness....

Do not, O LORD, withhold
   your mercy from me;
let your steadfast love and your faithfulness
   keep me safe forever.

PRAYER TO CARRY WITH ME

Psalm 40:6

…you have given me an open ear.

READING

Isaiah 43:18–21

Do not remember the former things,
    or consider the things of old.
I am about to do a new thing;
    now it springs forth, do you not perceive it?
I will make a way in the wilderness
    and rivers in the desert.
The wild animals will honor me,
    the jackals and the ostriches;
for I give water in the wilderness,
    rivers in the desert,
to give drink to my chosen people,
    the people whom I formed for myself
so that they might declare my praise.

RESPONSE

Psalm 98:1

O sing to the LORD a new song,
    for he has done marvelous things.

SILENT PRAYER FOR THE WORLD, OTHERS, AND OURSELVES

ACTION

Today, I have made a choice to seek one small area of my life
where I will "turn" and ask God to help me heal.

CONCLUDING PRAYER

The Liturgy of the Hours

Lord God, send peaceful sleep to refresh our tired bodies.
May your help always renew us and keep us strong in your
service. We ask this through Christ our Lord. Amen.

STATION 7 ~ *Jesus falls the second time*

ADDICTION ISSUES ~ *Slavery, discouragement,*
perseverance

 MORNING PRAYER

INVITATION TO PRAYER

O God of freedom, we are caught in spiritual bondage,
from cruelty and greed, failure of faith, deflated hope,
and loss of our connection with you. We hide our true
disappointments, diluting their sting with food or drink.
We covet others' happiness while refusing your invitation to
a whole, holy life. Please invite me again, Lord, and again.
Amen.

HYMN   *Go Down, Moses (African American Spiritual)*

When Israel was in Egypt Land,
   Let my people go!
Oppressed so hard they could not stand,
   Let my people go!
Go down Moses, way down in Egypt Land!
   Tell old Pharaoh, Let my people go!

When they had reached the other shore!
   Let my people go!
They sang a song of triumph o'er!
   Let my people go!
Go down, Moses, way down in Egypt Land!
   Tell old Pharaoh, Let my people go!

ANTIPHON   *Exodus 15:2*

The LORD is my strength and my might....

A song of Moses and the Israelites

The LORD is my strength and my might,
    and he has become my salvation;
this is my God, and I will praise him,
    my father's God, and I will exalt him.
The LORD is a warrior;
    the LORD is his name.

PRAYER TO CARRY WITH ME   *Exodus 15:2*
The LORD is my strength and my might…

READING   *Exodus 2, 3, 6–10 (adapted)*
In Egypt, the Israelites groaned under their slavery, and cried out…to God. God heard their groaning, and remembered his covenant with Abraham, Isaac, and Jacob (see Exodus 2).

"…I [will] come down to deliver them…and to bring them up out of that land to a good and broad land, a land flowing with milk and honey…(Exodus 3).

I know, however, that the king of Egypt will not let [them] go unless compelled by a mighty hand. So I will stretch out my hand and strike Egypt." Then the LORD said to Moses, "Now you shall see what I will do to Pharaoh….[and tell] the Israelites, '…I will redeem you with an outstretched arm and with mighty acts of judgment. I will take you as my people, and I will be your God….' " Moses told this to the Israelites; but they would not listen…because of their broken spirit and their cruel slavery (Exodus 6).

Blood

"…I will strike the water that is in the Nile, and it shall be turned to blood. The fish in the river shall die, the river itself shall stink, and the Egyptians shall be unable to drink water from the Nile…its rivers, its canals, and its ponds, and all its pools of water—[will] become blood; and there shall be blood throughout the whole land of Egypt, even in vessels of wood and in vessels of stone."

…and all the water in the river was turned into blood, and the fish in the river died. The river stank so that the Egyptians could not drink its water, and there was blood throughout the whole land of Egypt (Exodus 7).

Frogs

"…If you refuse to let them go, I will plague your whole country with frogs. The river shall swarm with frogs; they shall come up into your palace, into your bedchamber and your bed…and into your ovens and your kneading bowls." So…the frogs came up and covered the land of Egypt.

Then Pharaoh called Moses and Aaron, and said, "Pray to the LORD to take away the frogs from me and my people, and I will let the people go to sacrifice to the LORD."…And the LORD did as Moses requested: the frogs died in the houses, the courtyards, and the fields. And they gathered them together in heaps, and the land stank. But when Pharaoh saw that there was a respite, he hardened his heart, and would not listen to them, just as the LORD had said (Exodus 8).

Gnats

…"'strike the dust of the earth, so that it may become gnats throughout the whole land of Egypt.'"…and gnats came on humans and animals alike; all the dust of the earth turned into gnats throughout the whole land of Egypt....But Pharaoh's heart was hardened, and he would not listen to them, just as the Lord had said (Exodus 8).

Flies

"...if you will not let my people go, I will send swarms of flies on you"...and great swarms of flies came into the house of Pharaoh and...in all of Egypt the land was ruined because of the flies.

So Pharaoh said, "I will let you go to sacrifice to the LORD your God in the wilderness, provided you do not go very far away. Pray for me."

...and the LORD...removed the swarms of flies from Pharaoh...and from his people....But Pharaoh hardened his heart this time also, and would not let the people go (Exodus 8).

Pestilence

Then the LORD said..."Let my people go...if you refuse to let them go...[I] will strike with a deadly pestilence your livestock in the field: the horses, the donkeys, the camels, the herds, and the flocks." And on the next day the LORD did so; all the livestock of the Egyptians died....But the heart of Pharaoh was hardened, and he would not let the people go (Exodus 9).

Boils

Then the LORD said..."Take handfuls of soot from the kiln, and let Moses throw it in the air in the sight of Pharaoh. It shall become fine dust all over the land of Egypt, and shall cause festering boils on humans and animals throughout the whole land of Egypt." So they took soot from the kiln, and stood before Pharaoh, and Moses threw it in the air, and it caused festering boils on humans and animals....But the LORD hardened the heart of Pharaoh, and he would not listen to them, just as the LORD had spoken to Moses (Exodus 9).

Hail
Then the LORD said..."Thus says the LORD, the God of the Hebrews: Let my people go, so that they may worship me....Tomorrow at this time I will cause the heaviest hail to fall that has ever fallen in Egypt."...[then] the LORD sent thunder and hail, and fire came down...; there was hail with fire flashing continually in the midst of it....The hail struck down everything...both human and animal;...[and] all the plants of the field, and...every tree in the field....

Then Pharaoh...said..."This time I have sinned; the LORD is in the right, and I and my people are in the wrong. Pray to the LORD! Enough of God's thunder and hail! I will let you go; you need stay no longer."...But when Pharaoh saw that the rain and the hail and the thunder had ceased, he sinned once more and hardened his heart...and he would not let the Israelites go, just as the LORD had spoken through Moses (Exodus 9).

Locusts
"Thus says the LORD, the God of the Hebrews, 'How long will you refuse to humble yourself before me? Let my people go, so that they may worship me. For if you refuse to let my people go, tomorrow I will bring locusts into your country. ...They shall devour the last remnant left...after the hail, and...every tree of yours that grows in the field....' "

The locusts came upon all the land of Egypt...the land

was black; and they ate all the plants in the land and all the fruit of the trees that the hail had left; nothing green was left, no tree, no plant in the field, in all the land of Egypt. Pharaoh...said, "I have sinned against the LORD your God, and against you. Do forgive my sin just this once, and pray to the LORD your God that...he remove this deadly thing from me.'"...The LORD...lifted the locusts and drove them into the Red Sea....But the LORD hardened Pharaoh's heart, and he would not let the Israelites go (Exodus 10).

Darkness

Then the LORD said to Moses, "Stretch out your hand toward heaven so that there may be darkness over the land of Egypt, a darkness that can be felt."...and there was dense darkness in all the land of Egypt for three days. People could not see one another, and for three days they could not move from where they were....Then Pharaoh said, "Go, worship the LORD. Only your flocks and your herds shall remain behind. Even your children may go with you." But Moses said...."Our livestock also must go with us."...But the LORD hardened Pharaoh's heart, and he was unwilling to let them go (Exodus 11).

Death of the Firstborn

The LORD said, "I will bring one more plague upon Pharaoh and upon Egypt; afterwards he will let you go from here; indeed, when he lets you go, he will drive you away....

About midnight I will go...through Egypt. Every firstborn in the land of Egypt shall die, from the firstborn of Pharaoh who sits on his throne to the firstborn of the female slave who is behind the handmill, and all the firstborn of the livestock. Then there will be a loud cry throughout the whole land of Egypt, such as has never been nor will ever be again….[And they will say] "Leave us, you and all the people who follow you…" (Exodus 11).

RESPONSE

What am I willing to endure as the price for continuing my slavery in addiction? What are my ten plagues?

ACTION

Today, I will look for where in my life I am enslaved. Who is my master? An addictive substance or behavior? Abusive relationships? Lack of an adequate income? Jealousy and envy? An intractable physical problem? A battered soul?

CONCLUDING PRAYER

Lord, you have made us weak, so that we might know your strength. You have made us indecisive, so that we might know your unwavering faithfulness. Jesus said, "I am the way, the truth, and the life." Give us strength for the journey and steadfast confidence in your presence beside us. Amen.

 MIDDAY PRAYER

INVITATION TO PRAYER

O Lord our God, we praise and thank you for your power to free us when we create our own captivity, to sustain us each day with the bread of life, and to guide us every day to a new beginning. Amen.

HYMN *The God of Abraham Praise (v. 1, 6)*

The God of Abr'ham praise, / Who reigns enthroned above;
Ancient of everlasting days, / And God of love.
Jehovah, great I AM! / By earth and heav'n confessed;
I bow and bless the sacred name / Forever blest.

The goodly land I see, / With peace and plenty blest;
A land of sacred liberty, / And endless rest.
There milk and honey flow, / And oil and wine abound,
And trees of life forever grow / With mercy crowned.

ANTIPHON *Exodus 15:2*

The LORD is my strength and my might…

PSALM *Exodus 15:11, 13*

A song of Moses and the Israelites

"Who is like you, O LORD, among the gods?
    Who is like you, majestic in holiness,
awesome in splendor, doing wonders?

"In your steadfast love you led the people
    whom you redeemed;
    you guided them by your strength to your holy abode."

PRAYER TO CARRY WITH ME *Exodus 15:13*

"In your steadfast love you led the people whom you
redeemed.…"

READING *Exodus 12 (adapted)*

The LORD said to Moses…in the land of Egypt: Tell the
whole congregation of Israel that…they are to take a lamb
for each family, a lamb for each household…then the whole
assembled congregation of Israel shall slaughter it at twi-
light. They shall take some of the blood and put it on the
two doorposts and the lintel of the houses in which they
eat it. They shall eat the lamb that same night; they shall
eat it roasted over the fire with unleavened bread and bitter herbs.…This is how you shall eat it: your loins girded,
your sandals on your feet, and your staff in your hand; and

you shall eat it hurriedly. It is the passover of the LORD. For I will pass through the land of Egypt that night, and I will strike down every firstborn…both human beings and animals; on all the gods of Egypt I will execute judgments: I am the LORD. The blood shall be a sign for you on the houses where you live: when I see the blood, I will pass over you, and no plague shall destroy you when I strike the land of Egypt.

This day shall be a day of remembrance for you. You shall celebrate it as a festival to the LORD; throughout your generations you shall observe it as a perpetual ordinance.

Then Moses…said to them, "Go, select lambs for your families, and slaughter the passover lamb. Take a bunch of hyssop, dip it in the blood…in the basin, and touch the lintel and the two doorposts with the blood.…None of you shall go outside the door of your house until morning. For the LORD will pass through to strike down the Egyptians; when he sees the blood on the lintel and on the two doorposts, the LORD will pass over that door and will not allow the destroyer to enter your houses to strike you down. You shall observe this rite as a perpetual ordinance for you and your children.

The Israelites went and did just as the LORD had commanded.…

At midnight the LORD struck down all the firstborn in the land of Egypt, from the firstborn of Pharaoh who sat on his throne to the firstborn of the prisoner who was in the dungeon, and all the firstborn of the livestock.…and there was a loud cry in Egypt, for there was not a house without someone dead. Then [Pharaoh] summoned Moses…in the night, and said, "Rise up, go away from my people, both you and the Israelites! Go, worship the Lord, as you said. Take your flocks and your herds, as you said, and be gone. And bring a blessing on me too!"…

The Israelites journeyed [with] about six hundred thousand men on foot, besides children…and livestock in great numbers, both flocks and herds. They baked unleavened cakes of the dough…because they were driven out of Egypt and could not wait, nor had they prepared any provisions for themselves.…

That was for the LORD a night of vigil, to bring them out of the land of Egypt.

RESPONSE   *Exodus 13:1–2*

The LORD said to Moses: Consecrate to me all the firstborn; whatever is the first to open the womb among the Israelites, of human beings and animals, is mine.

Am I ready to consecrate my own life to God and to begin healing?

ACTION

Today, I will look for where in my life I am enslaved. Who is my master? An addictive substance or behavior? Abusive relationships? Lack of an adequate income? Jealousy and envy? An intractable physical problem? A battered soul?

CONCLUDING PRAYER

Lord, you have made us weak, so that we might know your strength. You have made us indecisive, so that we might know your unwavering faithfulness. Jesus said, "I am the way, the truth, and the life." Give us strength for the journey and steadfast confidence in your presence beside us. Amen.

INVITATION TO PRAYER

O Lord, open my lips and my mouth will declare your praise. Cleanse my heart of any worthless, evil, or distracting thoughts. Give me the energy and love to pray with attention, reverence, and devotion, and to let myself rest in your strength. Amen.

HYMN   *The God of Abraham Praise (v. 2, 4)*

The God of Abr'ham praise, / At whose supreme command
From earth I rise and seek the joys / At his right hand.
I all on earth forsake—Its wisdom, fame and pow'r—
And him my only portion make, / My shield and tow'r.

He by himself has sworn; / I on his oath depend.
I shall, on eagle wings upborne, / To heav'n ascend.
I shall behold his face; / I shall his pow'r adore,
And sing the wonders of his grace / For evermore.

ANTIPHON   *Exodus 14:14*

"The LORD will fight for you,
and you have only to keep still."

PSALM   *Exodus 15:1, 4, 5, 7, 8, 10*

A song of Moses and the Israelites

"I will sing to the LORD,
     for he has triumphed gloriously;
  horse and rider he has thrown into the sea....

"The floods covered them;
   they went down into the depths like a stone.
In the greatness of your majesty you overthrew
   your adversaries…*
   the deeps congealed in the heart of the sea.
You blew with your wind, the sea covered them;
   they sank like lead in the mighty waters."

PRAYER TO CARRY WITH ME   *Exodus 14:14*
"The LORD will fight for you, and you have only to keep still."

READING   *Exodus 14 (adapted)*
When the king of Egypt was told that the people had fled,
the minds of Pharaoh and his officials were changed…and
they said, "What have we done, letting Israel leave our
service?"…The LORD hardened the heart of Pharaoh and
he pursued the Israelites.…

   As Pharaoh drew near, the Israelites looked back, and
there were the Egyptians advancing on them. In great fear
the Israelites cried out to the LORD. They said to Moses,
"…it would have been better for us to serve the Egyptians
than to die in the wilderness." But Moses said to the people,
"Do not be afraid, stand firm, and see the deliverance that
the LORD will accomplish for you today.…The LORD will
fight for you, and you have only to keep still."

   Then the LORD said to Moses, "Tell the Israelites to go
forward. But…stretch out your hand over the sea and divide
it, that the Israelites may go into the sea on dry ground.
Then I will harden the hearts of the Egyptians so that they
will go in after them.…"

---

*Addictive substances and behaviors.

Then Moses stretched out his hand over the sea....The Israelites went into the sea on dry ground, the waters forming a wall for them on their right and on their left. The Egyptians pursued, and went into the sea after them....

Then the LORD said to Moses, "Stretch out your hand over the sea, so that the water may come back upon the Egyptians, upon their chariots and chariot drivers." So Moses stretched out his hand over the sea....The waters returned and covered the entire army of Pharaoh that had followed them into the sea; not one of them remained.

Thus, the LORD saved Israel that day from the Egyptians. So the people feared the LORD and believed in the LORD and in his servant Moses.

ACTION

Today, I will look for where in my life I am enslaved. Who is my master? An addictive substance or behavior? Abusive relationships? Lack of an adequate income? Jealousy and envy? An intractable physical problem? A battered soul?

CONCLUDING PRAYER

Lord, you have made us weak, so that we might know your strength. You have made us indecisive, so that we might know your unwavering faithfulness. Jesus said, "I am the way, the truth, and the life." Give us strength for the journey and steadfast confidence in your presence beside us. Amen.

INVITATION TO PRAYER

O Lord, your strength is above all strength, yet you fell, once, and then again. Help us trust in your strength when we are buffeted by desires and longings which promise relief, yet lead us deeper into darkness. Amen.

HYMN *O God of Jacob*

O God of Jacob, by whose hand
   your people still are fed,
who through this weary pilgrimage
   a wav'ring Israel led:

Our vows, our prayers, we now present
   before your throne of grace.
O God of Jacob, be the God
   of their succeeding race.

Through each perplexing path of life
   our wand'ring foot-steps guide;
give us this day our daily bread,
   and shelter fit provide.

Oh, grant us your protecting care
   till all our wand'rings cease
that to those mansions kept for us
   we all may come in peace.

**SILENT REFLECTION ON THE DAY
AND ON OURSELVES**

ANTIPHON *Our Father*

Lead us not into temptation, but deliver us from evil.

PSALM *Exodus 15:17–18*

A song of Moses and the Israelites

"You brought [your people] in and planted them on the
    mountain of your own possession,
  the place, O LORD, that you made your abode,
  the sanctuary, O LORD, that your hands have established.
The LORD will reign forever and ever."

PRAYER TO CARRY WITH ME *Our Father*

Lead us not into temptation, but deliver us from evil.

READING *Exodus 13:20–22 (adapted)*

They [the Israelites] set out…and camped…on the edge of
the wilderness. The LORD went in front of them in a pillar
of cloud by day, to lead them along the way, and in a pillar of
fire by night, to give them light, so that they might travel by
day and by night.…Neither the pillar of cloud by day nor the
pillar of fire by night left its place in front of the people.

RESPONSE

Lord, when we were born we did not get a map or set of
directions about how and where to live our lives. Bring into
my life guides whose direction is taken from you.

**SILENT PRAYER FOR THE WORLD,
OTHERS, AND OURSELVES**

ACTION

Today, I have looked for where, in my life, I live in slavery.
Continue to reveal to me, Lord, the ways in which I allow
anything, other than you, to be my master.

Lord, you have made us weak, so that we might know your strength. You have made us indecisive, so that we might know your unwavering faithfulness. Jesus said, "I am the way, the truth, and the life." Give us strength for the journey and steadfast confidence in your presence beside us. Amen.

STATION 8 ~ *Jesus meets the women of Jerusalem*

ADDICTION ISSUES ~ *Truth, courage, power*

 MORNING PRAYER

INVITATION TO PRAYER

O Lord, open my lips and my mouth will declare your praise. Cleanse my heart of any worthless, evil, or distracting thoughts. Give me the wisdom and love to pray with attention, reverence, and devotion. Guide my heart and my activity in the direction you would have them go to bring me healing and renewed energy. Amen.

HYMN   *Mothering God, You Gave Me Birth*

Mothering God, you gave me birth
in the morning of this world.
creator, source of ev'ry breath,
you are my rain, my wind, my sun.

Mothering Christ, you took my form,
offering me your food of light,
grain of new life, and grape of love,
your very body for my peace.

Mothering Spirit, nurt'ring one,
in arms of patience hold me close,
so that in faith I root and grow
until I flow'r, until I know.

"Come," my heart says, "seek his face!"
Your face, LORD, do I seek.

PSALM *Psalm 27:9–14*

Do not hide your face from me.
Do not turn your servant away in anger,
you who have been my help.
Do not cast me off, do not forsake me,
O God of my salvation!
If my father and mother forsake me,
the LORD will take me up.

Teach me your way, O Lord,
and lead me on a level path
because of my enemies
[all addictive substances and behaviors].
Do not give me up to the will of my adversaries,
for false witnesses have risen against me,
and they are breathing out violence.

I believe that I shall see the goodness of the LORD
in the land of the living.
Wait for the LORD;
be strong, and let your heart take courage;
wait for the LORD!

PRAYER TO CARRY WITH ME *Psalm 27:8*

"Come," my heart says, "seek his face!"
Your face, LORD, do I seek.

READING *Mark 16:9–11; {John 20:14–16}; (Luke 24:11)*

Now after [Jesus] rose early on the first day of the week, he appeared first to Mary Magdalene, from whom he had cast out seven demons. {She turned around and saw Jesus standing there, but she did not know that it was Jesus. Jesus said to her, "Woman, why are you weeping? Whom are you looking for?" Supposing him to be the gardener, she said to him, "Sir, if you have carried him away, tell me where you have laid him, and I will take him away." Jesus said to her, "Mary!" She…said to him in Hebrew, "Rabbouni!" (which means Teacher).} She went out and told those who had been with him, while they were mourning and weeping. But when they heard that he was alive and had been seen by her (*these words seemed to them an idle tale, and*)…they would not believe it.

RESPONSE

Where in my life have I been unfairly discredited or stigmatized? Why? Sexism, racism, ageism, others' jealousy, my own weaknesses? What addictive behaviors or substances have I used to numb that emotional assault and bury the anger?

ACTION

Today, I will look for a new beginning in one place, or one person in my life. Without combativeness, I will speak the truth and not allow myself to be discounted.

CONCLUDING PRAYER *From "On the Pulse of Morning"*

Lift up your eyes
Upon this day breaking for you.
Give birth again
To the dream.

Women, children, men,
Take it into the palms of your hands,
Mold it into the shape of your most
Private need. Sculpt it into
The image of your most public self.
Lift up your hearts
Each new hour holds new chances
For [a new beginning.]
Do not be wedded forever
To fear, yoked eternally
To brutishness.

The horizon leans forward,
Offering you space to place new steps of change
Here, on the pulse of this fine day
You may have the courage
To look up and out and upon me,
The Rock, the River, the Tree, your country.
No less to Midas than to the mendicant.
No less to you now than the mastodon then.

Here on the pulse of this new day
You may have the grace to look up and out
And into your sister's eyes,
And into your brother's face, your country,
And say simply
Very simply
With hope—
Good morning.

MAYA ANGELOU

INVITATION TO PRAYER

O God of strength, show me what I need to do to escape the prison of my addictions. Lead me to the source of your healing, and give me the courage to ask for it. Draw my attention to the little pockets of time and space where you dwell, ready to offer me everything I need, and more, to fill the emptiness I carry within myself. Amen.

HYMN *My Song Is Love Unknown (v. 1, 3, 4)*

My song is love unknown, / My Savior's love to me,
Love to the loveless shown, / That they might lovely be.
Oh, who am I, that for my sake / My Lord should take frail
flesh and die? / My Lord should take frail flesh and die?

Sometimes they strew his way / And his sweet praises sing;
Resounding all the day / Hosannas to their King.
Then "Crucify!" is all their breath, / And for his death
they thirst and cry. / And for his death they thirst and cry.

Why, what hath my Lord done?
   What makes this rage and spite?
He made the lame to run, / He gave the blind their sight.
Sweet injuries! Yet they at these / Themselves displease,
and 'gainst him rise; / Themselves displease,
   and 'gainst him rise.

ANTIPHON *Psalm 72:12*

[H]e delivers…those who have no helper.

PSALM

Psalm 72:12–14

For he delivers the needy when they call,
  the poor and those who have no helper.
He has pity on the weak and the needy,
  and saves the lives of the needy.
From oppression and violence he redeems their life;
  and precious is their blood in his sight.

PRAYER TO CARRY WITH ME

Psalm 72:12

[H]e delivers...those who have no helper.

READING

Mark 5:25–34

Now there was a woman who had been suffering from hemorrhages for twelve years. She had endured much under many physicians, and had spent all that she had; she was no better, but rather grew worse. She had heard about Jesus, and came up behind him in the crowd and touched his cloak, for she said, "If I but touch his clothes, I will be made well." Immediately her hemorrhage stopped; and she felt in her body that she was healed of her disease. Immediately aware that power had gone forth from him, Jesus turned about in the crowd and said, "Who touched my clothes?" He looked all around to see who had done it. But the woman, knowing what had happened to her, came in fear and trembling, fell down before him, and told him the whole truth. He said to her, "Daughter, your faith has made you well; go in peace, and be healed of your disease."

RESPONSE

Isaiah 54:4a

"Do not fear, for you will not be ashamed;
  do not be discouraged, for you will not suffer disgrace."

ACTION

Where in my life do I feel humiliated and shamed? Today, I will look for a new beginning in one place, or one person in my life. Without combativeness, I will speak the truth and not allow myself to be unfairly discounted.

CONCLUDING PRAYER

Lord, you have made us weak, so that we might know your strength. You have let us become ill, so that we might know the power of your healing. Jesus says, "I am the way, the truth, and the life." Give our broken bodies and spirits strength for the journey and steadfast confidence in your presence beside us. Amen.

 EVENING PRAYER

INVITATION TO PRAYER

O God of strength, I am strong, but I lose my focus. The workday is a whirlwind of noise, activity, and demands. I forget that I have the power to change or leave what is toxic to my spirit and drives me to self-destructive behavior. Remind me of my strength and that it all comes from you. Lord, help me to reclaim my energy and my life. Amen.

HYMN
I Was There to Hear Your Borning Cry (John C. Ylvisaker)

I was there to hear your borning cry,
  I'll be there when you are old.
I rejoiced the day you were baptized
  to see your life unfold.

I was there when you were but a child,
    with a faith to suit you well;
In a blaze of light you wandered off
    to find where demons dwell.

In the middle ages of your life,
    not too old, no longer young,
I'll be there to guide you through the night,
    complete what I've begun.

When the evening gently closes in
    and you shut your weary eyes,
I'll be there as I have always been
    with just one more surprise.

I was there to hear your borning cry,
    I'll be there when you are old.
I rejoiced the day you were baptized,
    to see your life unfold.

ANTIPHON   *Psalm 31:4*
…take me out of the net that is hidden for me,
    for you are my refuge.

PSALM   *Psalm 31:1–5*
In you, O LORD, I seek refuge;
    do not let me ever be put to shame;
    in your righteousness deliver me.
Incline your ear to me;
    rescue me speedily.
Be a rock of refuge for me,
    a strong fortress to save me.

You are indeed my rock and my fortress;

for your name's sake lead me and guide me,

take me out of the net that is hidden for me,

for you are my refuge.

Into your hand I commit my spirit;

you have redeemed me, O LORD, faithful God.

PRAYER TO CARRY WITH ME   *Psalm 31:4*

…take me out of the net that is hidden for me,

for you are my refuge.

READING   *Genesis 29:16–30*

Now Laban had two daughters; the name of the elder was
Leah, and the name of the younger was Rachel. Leah's eyes
were lovely, and Rachel was graceful and beautiful. Jacob
loved Rachel; so he said [to Laban] "I will serve you seven
years for your younger daughter Rachel." Laban said, "It is
better that I give her to you than that I should give her to any
other man; stay with me." So Jacob served seven years for
Rachel, and they seemed to him but a few days because of
the love he had for her.

Then Jacob said to Laban, "Give me my wife that I may
go in to her, for my time is completed." So Laban gathered
together all the people of the place, and made a feast. But
in the evening he took his daughter Leah and brought her
to Jacob; and he went in to her.…When morning came, it
was Leah! And Jacob said to Laban, "What is this you have
done to me? Did I not serve with you for Rachel? Why then
have you deceived me?" Laban said, "This is not done in our
country—giving the younger before the firstborn. Complete
the [bridal] week of this one, and we will give you the other
also in return for serving me another seven years." Jacob did

so, and completed her [bridal] week; then Laban gave him his daughter Rachel as a wife....So Jacob went in to Rachel also, and he loved Rachel more than Leah. He served Laban for another seven years.

RESPONSE   *Isaiah 54:5, 6*

"For your Maker is your husband,
    the LORD of hosts is his name....
For the LORD has called you
    like a wife forsaken and grieved in spirit,
like the wife of a man's youth when she is cast off,"
    says your God.

ACTION

Where in my life have I felt marginalized or rejected? Today, I will look for a new beginning in one place, or one person in my life. Without combativeness, I will speak the truth and not allow myself to be discounted.

CONCLUDING PRAYER

Lord, protect me from investing the best part of my love in things of this world. Show me how to reserve that part for you. Take away my fear of what is real and cannot be changed. Teach me to recognize your greatest gift to me, the wholeness of my self. Hold me in your light so that I can see myself as you see me. Amen.

INVITATION TO PRAYER

O generous God, you invite us to life and give us the gift of ourselves. We are "fearfully and wonderfully made" and yet we squander our time, our talents, our energy on things that deplete us and fill up the open space between us. Draw us close, and remind us that in you, we are already healed. Amen.

HYMN   *Awake, O Sleeper (v. 1, 2, 4, 5)*

Awake, O sleeper, rise from death,
And Christ shall give you light
So learn his love—its length and breadth,
Its fullness, depth, and height.

To us on earth he came to bring
From sin and fear release,
To give the Spirit's unity
The very bond of peace.

Then walk in love as Christ has loved
Who died that he might save;
With kind and gentle hearts forgive,
As God in Christ forgave.

For us Christ lived, for us he died
And conquered in the strife.
Awake, arise, go forth in faith,
And Christ shall give you life.

**SILENT REFLECTION ON THE DAY
AND ON OURSELVES**

...you heard my supplications
  when I cried out to you for help.

PSALM *Psalm 126:1–7*

When the LORD restored the fortunes of Zion,
  we were like those who dream.
Then our mouth was filled with laughter,
  and our tongue with shouts of joy;
then it was said among the nations,
  "The LORD has done great things for them."
The LORD has done great things for us,
  and we rejoiced.

Restore our fortunes, O LORD,
  like the watercourses in the Negeb.
May those who sow in tears
  reap with shouts of joy.
Those who go out weeping,
  bearing the seed for sowing,
shall come home with shouts of joy,
  carrying their sheaves.

PRAYER TO CARRY WITH ME *Psalm 31:22*

...you heard my supplications
  when I cried out to you for help.

READING *Luke 13:10–17*

Now [Jesus] was teaching in one of the synagogues on the
sabbath. And just then there appeared a woman with a spirit
that had crippled her for eighteen years. She was bent over
and was quite unable to stand up straight. When Jesus saw
her, he called her over and said, "Woman, you are set free

from your ailment." When he laid his hands on her, immediately she stood up straight and began praising God. But the leader of the synagogue, indignant because Jesus had cured on the sabbath, kept saying to the crowd, "There are six days on which work ought to be done; come on those days and be cured, and not on the sabbath day." But the Lord answered him and said, "You hypocrites! Does not each of you on the sabbath untie his ox or his donkey from the manger, and lead it away to give it water? And ought not this woman, a daughter of Abraham whom Satan bound for eighteen long years, be set free from this bondage on the sabbath day?" When he said this, all his opponents were put to shame; and the entire crowd was rejoicing at all the wonderful things that he was doing.

RESPONSE
Who or what has a vested interest in my staying addicted, codependent, shamed, weak, unproductive, powerless?

SILENT PRAYER FOR THE WORLD, OTHERS, AND OURSELVES

Our Father

Our Father, who art in heaven, hallowed be thy name;
    thy kingdom come, thy will be done on earth as it is in
    heaven.
Give us this day our daily bread; and forgive us our
    trespasses, as we forgive those who trespass against us;
and lead us not into temptation, but deliver us from evil.
    For the kingdom, the power, and the glory are yours
    now and for ever. Amen.

ACTION

Today, I have looked for a new beginning in one place, or one person in my life. Without combativeness, I will begin to speak the truth and not allow myself to be unfairly discounted.

CONCLUDING PRAYER *The Liturgy of the Hours*

Protect us, Lord, as we stay awake;
   watch over us as we sleep,
that awake, we may keep watch
   with Christ,
and asleep, rest in his peace. Amen.

STATION 9 ~ *Jesus falls a third time*

ADDICTION ISSUES ~ *Temptation, danger, forgetting*

 MORNING PRAYER

INVITATION TO PRAYER

O Lord, open my lips and my mouth will declare your praise. Give me strength to pray with the expectation of your presence and energy to resist the temptations which will seek me out today. Help me to make good choices, ones that give life, not take it. Amen.

HYMN *Lost in the Night (v. 1, 3)*

Lost in the night do the people yet languish
Longing for morning and darkness to vanquish,
Plaintively heaving a sigh full of anguish,
Will not day come soon? Will not day come soon?

Sorrowing wand'rers, in darkness yet dwelling,
Dawned has the day of a radiance excelling,
Death's dreaded darkness forever dispelling.
Christ is coming soon! Christ is coming soon!

ANTIPHON *Psalm 40:11*

…let your steadfast love and faithfulness
keep me safe forever.

PSALM *Psalm 40:11–12*
A psalm for Jacob

Do not, O LORD, withhold
your mercy from me;

let your steadfast love and your faithfulness
    keep me safe forever.
For evils have encompassed me
    without number;
my iniquities have overtaken me,
    until I cannot see;
they are more than the hairs of my head,
    and my heart fails me.

PRAYER TO CARRY WITH ME   *Psalm 40:11*

…let your steadfast love and faithfulness
    keep me safe forever.

READING   *Genesis 25:19—28:9 (paraphrased)*

Isaac was sixty years old when Rebekah gave birth to twins.
The first came out red, all his body like a hairy mantle;
so they named him Esau. Afterward his brother came out,
with his hand gripping Esau's heel; so he was named Jacob.

When the boys grew up, Esau was a skillful hunter,
a man of the field, while Jacob was a quiet man, living in
tents. Isaac loved Esau, because he was fond of game; but
Rebekah loved Jacob.

Once when Jacob was cooking a stew, Esau came in from
the field, and he was famished. Esau said to Jacob, "Let me
eat some of that red stuff, for I am famished!"…Jacob said,
"First sell me your birthright."… So he swore to him, and
sold his birthright to Jacob. Then Jacob gave Esau bread and
lentil stew, and he ate and drank, and rose and went his way.
Thus Esau despised his birthright.…

When Isaac was old and his eyes were dim so that he
could not see, he called his elder son Esau and said to him,
"My son…I am old; I do not know the day of my death.

Now then, take your weapons…and go out to the field, and hunt game for me. Then prepare for me savory food…and bring it to me to eat, so that I may bless you before I die."

Now Rebekah was listening when Isaac spoke to his son Esau. So when Esau went to the field to hunt for game and bring it, Rebekah said to her son Jacob, "I heard your father say to your brother Esau, 'Bring me game, and prepare for me savory food to eat, that I may bless you before the LORD before I die.' Therefore, my son, go to the flock, and get me two choice kids, so that I may prepare from them savory food for your father, such as he likes; and you shall take it to your father to eat, so that he may bless you before he dies."… So he went and got them and brought them to his mother; and his mother prepared savory food, such as his father loved. Then Rebekah took the best garments of her elder son Esau, which were with her in the house, and put them on her younger son Jacob; and she put the skins of the kids on his hands and on the smooth part of his neck.…

So he went in to his father, and then Isaac said to Jacob, "Come near, that I may feel you, my son, to know whether you are really my son Esau or not." So Jacob went up to his father Isaac, who felt him and said, "The voice is Jacob's voice, but the hands are the hands of Esau." He did not recognize him, because his hands were hairy like his brother Esau's.…Then his father Isaac said to him, "Come near and kiss me, my son." So he came near and kissed him; and he smelled the smell of his garments, and blessed him, and said, "Ah, the smell of my son is like the smell of a field that the LORD has blessed. May God give you of the dew of heaven, and of the fatness of the earth, and plenty of grain and wine. Let peoples serve you, and nations bow down to you. Be lord over your brothers, and may your mother's sons bow down to you. Cursed be everyone who curses you, and blessed be everyone who blesses you!"

As soon as Isaac had finished blessing Jacob...his brother Esau came in from his hunting....His father Isaac said to him, "Who are you?" He answered, "I am your firstborn son, Esau." Then Isaac trembled violently, and said, "Who was it then that hunted game and brought it to me, and I ate it all before you came, and I have blessed him?...Esau heard his father's words [and] cried out with a great and bitter cry, "Bless me, also, father!" But Isaac said, "Your brother came deceitfully, and he has taken away your blessing....I have already made him your lord, and I have given him all his brothers as servants, and with grain and wine I have sustained him."...Esau wept. Then his father said, "See, away from the fatness of the earth shall your home be, and away from the dew of heaven on high. By your sword you shall live, and you shall serve your brother; but when you break loose, you shall break his yoke from your neck."

Now Esau hated Jacob...and said to himself, "I will kill my brother Jacob." But the words of her elder son Esau were told to Rebekah; so she sent and called her younger son Jacob and said, "Your brother Esau is consoling himself by planning to kill you....flee at once to my brother Laban... and stay with until your brother's fury turns away...then I will send and bring you back from there....

Then Isaac called Jacob and blessed him..."May God Almighty bless you and make you fruitful and numerous.... May he give to you the blessing of Abraham, to you and to your offspring."...Thus Isaac sent Jacob away.

How have I deceived myself about the consequences
when I have been unable to resist temptation?

ACTION
Today, I will notice when I distort the truth, even just a little,
and when I twist the facts to suit my purposes.

CONCLUDING PRAYER
Lord, you have taught me what I need to know about resisting temptation, and about the devastating consequences,
for myself and those I love, when I turn away from your
generosity. You have made sure that there is "enough" to go
around, that I do not need to feel or act out of scarcity,
but rather out of the abundance you have already given me.
Help me to remember. Amen.

 MIDDAY PRAYER

INVITATION TO PRAYER
O Lord, Holy Spirit, you speak to us in stories from the past
about temptations and desires we have in the present. We
forget these lessons when the pleasures of this world seduce
us. Help me remember, Lord, that you also battled temptation in the desert. If I can remember your struggle, I can
draw on your strength. Help me to make good choices, out of
love for you, myself, and others. Amen.

HYMN   *Oh, Come, Oh, Come, Emmanuel (v. 1, 2)*
Oh, come, oh, come, Emmanuel,
And ransom captive Israel,
That mourns in lonely exile here
Until the Son of God appear.

Rejoice! Rejoice! Emmanuel
Shall come to you, O Israel.

Oh, come, oh, come, great Lord of might,
Who to your tribes on Sinai's height
In ancient times once gave the law
In cloud, in majesty, and awe.

Rejoice! Rejoice! Emmanuel
Shall come to you, O Israel.

ANTIPHON   *Psalm 78:18*
They tested God in their heart
   by demanding the food they craved.

PSALM *Psalm 78:10, 17–18, 20–22, 29, 35–38, 40–41, 58*
[The Israelites] did not keep God's covenant,
   but refused to walk according to his law.…

[T]hey sinned still more against him
   rebelling against the Most High in the desert.
They tested God in their heart
   by demanding the food they craved.
They spoke against God, saying…
"Even though he struck the rock so that water gushed out
   and torrents overflowed,
can he also give bread,
   or provide meat for his people?"
Therefore, when the LORD heard, he was full of rage;
   a fire was kindled against Jacob,
   his anger mounted against Israel,
because they had no faith in God,
   and did not trust his saving power.…

[The Israelites] ate and were well filled,
    for [God] gave them what they craved.…

In spite of all this they still sinned;
    they did not believe in his wonders.
They remembered that God was their rock,
    the Most High God their redeemer.
But they flattered him with their mouths;
    they lied to him with their tongues.
Their heart was not steadfast toward him;
    they were not true to his covenant.
Yet he, being compassionate,
    forgave their iniquity,
    and did not destroy them;
often he restrained his anger,
    and did not stir up all his wrath.
How often they rebelled against him in the wilderness
    and grieved him in the desert!
They tested God again and again,
    and provoked the Holy One of Israel.

…they provoked him to anger [and]…
    …moved him to jealousy with their idols.

PRAYER TO CARRY WITH ME   *Psalm 78:29*
[The Israelites] ate and were well filled,
    for he gave them what they craved.

READING   *Exodus 32:1–10*
When the people saw that Moses delayed to come down from the mountain [Mount Sinai], the people gathered around Aaron, and said to him, "Come, make gods for us, who shall go before us; as for this Moses, the man who brought us up

out of the land of Egypt, we do not know what has become of him." Aaron said to them, "Take off the gold rings that are on the ears of your wives, your sons, and your daughters, and bring them to me." So all the people took off the gold rings from their ears, and brought them to Aaron. He took the gold from them, formed it in a mold, and cast an image of a calf; and they said, "These are your gods, O Israel, who brought you up out of the land of Egypt!" When Aaron saw this, he built an altar before it; and Aaron made proclamation and said, "Tomorrow shall be a festival to the LORD." They rose early the next day, and offered burnt offerings and brought sacrifices of well-being; and the people sat down to eat and drink, and rose up to revel.

The LORD said to Moses, "Go down at once! Your people, whom you brought up out of the land of Egypt, have acted perversely; they have been quick to turn aside from the way that I commanded them; they have cast for themselves an image of a calf, and have worshiped it and sacrificed to it, and said, 'These are your gods, O Israel, who brought you up out of the land of Egypt!' The LORD said to Moses, "I have seen this people, how stiff-necked they are. Now let me alone, so that my wrath may burn hot against them and I may consume them...."

RESPONSE

How do I make "idols" out of things that belong in the economy of this world, not in God's economy? What do I "worship"? Money, beauty, power? Living in the "right" neighborhood, knowing all the inside gossip of my community? What *are* the consequences when I have been unable to resist these temptations?

ACTION

Today, I will notice when I distort the truth, even just a little, and when I twist the facts to suit my purposes.

CONCLUDING PRAYER

Lord, you taught me what I need to know about resisting temptation—and the devastating consequences, for me and those I love, when I turn away from your generosity. You make sure there is "enough" to go around; I do not need to feel or act out of scarcity, but rather out of the abundance you have given me. Help me to remember. Amen.

 EVENING PRAYER

INVITATION TO PRAYER

O Lord, Holy Spirit, you speak to us in stories from the past about temptations and desires we have in the present. We learn these lessons, but forget them when the pleasures of this world seek and seduce us. Teach me to practice making good choices, and to remember that, in repentance, when I ask for your forgiveness, you will give it. Amen.

HYMN   *The King of Love My Shepherd Is*

The King of love, my shepherd is,
Whose goodness faileth never;
I nothing lack if I am his
And he is mine forever.

Perverse and foolish oft I strayed,
But yet in love he sought me,
And on his shoulder gently laid,
At home, rejoicing, brought me.

Create in me a clean heart, O God,
   and put a new and right spirit within me.

PSALM *Psalm 51:1–2, 6–7, 10, 12*
*A psalm of David...after [he] had committed adultery
with Bathsheba*

Have mercy on me, O God,
   according to your steadfast love;
according to your abundant mercy
   blot out my transgressions.
Wash me thoroughly from my iniquity,
   and cleanse me from my sin....

You desire truth in the inward being;
   therefore teach me wisdom in my secret heart.
Purge me with hyssop, and I shall be clean;
   wash me, and I shall be whiter than snow.

Create in me a clean heart, O God,
   and put a new and right spirit within me....
Restore to me the joy of your salvation,
   and sustain in me a willing spirit.

PRAYER TO CARRY WITH ME *Psalm 51:10*
Create in me a clean heart, O God,
and put a new and right spirit within me.

READING *2 Samuel 11:1–5, 14–16, 18, 24, 26–27*
In the spring of the year, the time when kings go out
to battle, David sent...his officers and all Israel [and
they] ravaged...and besieged [their enemies]. But David
remained at Jerusalem.

It happened late one afternoon, when David rose from his couch and was walking about on the roof of the king's house, that he saw from the roof a woman bathing; the woman was very beautiful. David sent someone to inquire about the woman. It was reported, "This is Bathsheba...the wife of Uriah the Hittite." So David sent messengers to get her, and she came to him, and he lay with her....Then she returned to her house. The woman conceived; and she sent and told David, "I am pregnant...."

In the morning David wrote a letter to Joab [his commander]....In the letter he wrote, "Set Uriah in the forefront of the hardest fighting, and then draw back from him, so that he may be struck down and die." As Joab was besieging the city, he assigned Uriah to the place where he knew there were valiant warriors....Then Joab sent and told David all the news about the fighting; and [y]our servant Uriah the Hittite is dead too."

When the wife of Uriah heard that her husband was dead, she made lamentation for him. When the mourning was over, David sent and brought her to his house, and she became his wife, and bore him a son.

RESPONSE   *Isaiah 43:25*

I, I am He
    who blots out your transgressions for my own sake,
    and I will not remember your sins.

ACTION

How have I deceived myself about the consequences when I have been unable to resist temptation? Today, I will notice when I distort the truth, even just a little.

Concluding Prayer

Lord, you have taught me what I need to know about resisting temptation, and about the devastating consequences when I turn away from your love; when I seek gratification in others, and not in you. Thank you for this day and for yourself. Send rest to my body and calm to my soul, so that I will have the energy and commitment to remember to seek you first. Amen.

 ## NIGHT PRAYER

Invitation to Prayer

O Lord, let my prayer rise before you as incense, lifting up my voice to the evening and to you. Calm my heart and still my racing thoughts. Take from me the regrets, fatigue, and carelessness of my day, and remind me again that only you can bring me the peace that passes all understanding. Stay close, dear Lord, and help me. Amen.

Hymn   *The King of Love My Shepherd Is (v. 2, 5, 4)*

Where streams of living water flow,
My ransomed soul he leadeth
And, where the verdant pastures grow,
With food celestial feedeth.

Thou spreadst a table in my sight;
Thine unction grace bestoweth;
And, oh, what transport of delight
From thy pure chalice floweth!

In death's dark vale I fear no ill,
With thee, dear Lord, beside me,
Thy rod and staff my comfort still;
Thy cross before to guide me.

SILENT REFLECTION ON THE DAY AND ON OURSELVES

ANTIPHON
Psalm 63:7

...for you have been my help...

PSALM
Psalm 63:5–7

My soul is satisfied as with a rich feast,
and my mouth praises you with joyful lips
when I think of you...
and meditate on you in the watches of the night;
for you have been my help,
and in the shadow of your wings I sing for joy.

PRAYER TO CARRY WITH ME
Psalm 63:7

...for you have been my help...

READING
Romans 14:13, 15, 17, 19–21

Let us therefore no longer pass judgment on one another,
but resolve instead never to put a stumbling block or hindrance
in the way of another....If your brother or sister is
being injured by what you eat, you are no longer walking in
love. Do not let what you eat cause the ruin of one for whom
Christ died....For the kingdom of God is not food and drink
but righteousness and peace and joy in the Holy Spirit.
Let us then pursue what makes for peace and for mutual
[support]. Do not, for the sake of food, destroy the work of
God...it is wrong for you to make others fall by what you eat;
it is good not to eat meat or drink wine or do anything that
makes your brother or sister stumble.

RESPONSE

Have I considered the effect I have on others by what I eat or drink? Not that I cause them trouble or distress, but that others might use my behavior as a model to begin eating or drinking destructively?

SILENT PRAYER FOR THE WORLD, OTHERS, AND OURSELVES

ACTION

Today, I have tried to notice when I distort the truth, even just a little. I have deceived myself about the consequences when I cannot resist satisfying my insatiable hungers for food, drink, sex, or money. But, there is also the craving to shade things to my advantage, to look good in front of other people. The truth is, Lord, I forget you are there too, watching me trade my wholeness for instant gratification. Help me to be more aware.

CONCLUDING PRAYER

God of rest, we wander as aimlessly as sheep, distracted by this sparkling world, always looking for more, but needing less. Shepherd us back to your fold where you have laid a feast for us, where "streams of living water flow" and you are there beside us. Amen.

STATION 10 ~ *Jesus is stripped of his garments*

ADDICTION ISSUES ~ *Humiliation, shame, failure*

 MORNING PRAYER

INVITATION TO PRAYER

O Lord, open my lips and my mouth will declare your praise. Cleanse my heart of any self-serving, arrogant, or distracting thoughts. Send down to those who love you and would obey your commandments the discernment to separate the seductiveness of this world from the beauty of your kingdom. In Jesus' name. Amen.

HYMN *Your Hand, O Lord, in Days of Old (v. 1–3)*

Your hand, O Lord, in days of old
  Was strong to heal and save;
It triumphed oe'r disease and death,
  O'er darkness and the grave.
To you they came, the blind, the dumb,
  The palsied and the lame,
The lepers in their misery
  The sick with fevered frame.

And lo, your touch brought life and health,
  Gave speech and strength and sight;
And youth renewed and frenzy calmed
  Revealed you, Lord of light;
And now, O Lord, be near to bless,
  Almighty as before,
In crowded street, by beds of pain,
  As by Gennes'ret's shore.

Oh, be our great deliverer still,
    The Lord of life and death;
Restore and quicken, soothe and bless,
    With your life-giving breath.
To hands that work and eyes that see
    Give wisdom's healing power,
That whole and sick and weak and strong
    May praise you evermore.

ANTIPHON   *Psalm 10:12*

Rise up, O LORD; O God, lift up your hand;
    do not forget the oppressed.

PSALM   *Psalm 12:5–8*

"Because the poor are [oppressed],
        because the needy groan,
    I will now rise up," says the LORD;
"I will place them in the safety for which they long."
The promises of the LORD are promises that are pure
    silver refined in a furnace on the ground,
        purified seven times.

You, O LORD, will protect us;
    you will guard us from this generation forever.
On every side the wicked prowl,
    as vileness is exalted among humankind.

PRAYER TO CARRY WITH ME   *Psalm 10:12*

Rise up, O LORD; O God, lift up your hand;
    do not forget the oppressed.

READING

Mark 1:32–39

That evening, at sundown, they brought to him all who were sick or possessed with demons. And the whole city was gathered around the door. And he cured many who were sick with various diseases, and cast out many demons; and he would not permit the demons to speak, because they knew him.

In the morning, while it was still very dark, he got up and went out to a deserted place, and there he prayed. And Simon and his companions hunted for him. When they found him, they said to him, "Everyone is searching for you." He answered, "Let us go on to the neighboring towns, so that I may proclaim the message there also; for that is what I came out to do." And he went throughout Galilee, proclaiming the message in their synagogues and casting out demons.

RESPONSE

Psalm 43:3

O send out your light and your truth;
   let them lead me;
let them bring me to your holy hill
   and to your dwelling.

ACTION

Today I will search for my personal demons. How do my behavior, the choices I make, and my unwillingness to tell the truth enable them to keep me enslaved?

CONCLUDING PRAYER

Lord, all your ways are peace, and you welcome those who love you. Guide us so that we will turn our hearts to you. In peace let us pray to the Lord. Lord, have mercy. Amen.

INVITATION TO PRAYER

O Lord, your strength is above all strength. You experienced humiliation and shame so that we don't have to; you invite us to throw our sins into your grave, and then to rise with you. We are vain, prideful, and arrogant when we refuse your invitation to give our lives to you. Please, come with me to the cave of my heart and destroy the legion of demons that have kept me enslaved. In Jesus' name. Amen.

HYMN *Where Restless Crowds Are Thronging*

Where restless crowds are thronging Along the city ways,
Where pride and greed and turmoil
    Consume the fevered days,
Where vain ambitions banish
    All thoughts of praise and prayer,
The people's spirits waver: But you, O Christ, are there.

In scenes of want and sorrow And haunts of flagrant wrong,
In homes where kindness falters,
    And strife and fear are strong,
In busy streets of barter In lonely thoroughfare,
The people's spirits languish: But you, O Christ, are there.

With bombing and fierce burning Your people find no peace.
Help us to share their yearning That senseless death will cease.
Break through our ease and comfort, Forbid that we not care;
And strengthen all our efforts, For you, O Christ, are there.

O Christ, behold your people; They press on every hand!
Bring light to all the cities Of our divided land.

May all our bitter striving Give way to visions fair
Of righteousness and justice, For you, O Christ, are there.

ANTIPHON   *Psalm 102:24*

"O my God," I say, "do not take me away
   at the mid-point of my life...."

PSALM   *Psalm 102:1–9, 11*

Hear my prayer, O LORD;
   let my cry come to you.
Do not hide your face from me
   in the day of my distress.
Incline your ear to me;
   answer me speedily in the day when I call.

For my days pass away like smoke,
   and my bones burn like a furnace.
My heart is stricken and withered like grass;
   I am too wasted to eat my bread.
Because of my loud groaning
   my bones cling to my skin.
I am like an owl of the wilderness,
   like a little owl of the waste places.
I lie awake;
   I am like a lonely bird on the housetop.
All day long my enemies taunt me;
   those who deride me use my name for a curse.
For I eat ashes like bread,
   and mingle tears with my drink....
My days are like an evening shadow;
   I wither away like grass.

"O my God," I say, "do not take me away
    at the mid-point of my life…."

Reading   *Mark 5:1–15, 17–20*

[Jesus] came to the other side of the sea, to the country of
the Gerasenes. And when he had stepped out of the boat,
immediately a man out of the tombs with an unclean spirit
met him. He lived among the tombs; and no one could
restrain him any more, even with a chain; for he had often
been restrained with shackles and chains, but the chains he
wrenched apart, and the shackles he broke in pieces; and no
one had the strength to subdue him. Night and day among
the tombs and on the mountains he was always howling and
bruising himself with stones. When he saw Jesus from a
distance, he ran and bowed down before him; and he shout-
ed at the top of his voice, "What have you to do with me,
Jesus, Son of the Most High God? I swear to you by God, do
not torment me." For [Jesus] had said to him, "Come out of
the man, you unclean spirit!" Then Jesus asked [the unclean
spirit], "What is your name?" [The demon] replied, "My
name is Legion;* for we are many." He begged [Jesus] ear-
nestly not to send them out of the country [into the Abyss,
or Hell]. Now there on the hillside a great herd of swine was
feeding; and the unclean spirits begged him, "Send us into
the swine; let us enter them." So he gave them permission.
And the unclean spirits came out and entered the swine; and
the herd, numbering about two thousand, rushed down the
steep bank into the sea, and were drowned in the sea.

---

*A Roman legion consisted of six thousand men. Here the term
suggests that the man was possessed by numerous demons and perhaps
also represents the many powers opposed to Jesus (*NIV*, p. 1501).

The swineherds ran off and told it in the city and in the country. Then people came to see what it was that had happened. They came to Jesus and saw the demoniac sitting there, clothed and in his right mind, the very man who had had the legion; and they were afraid….Then they began to beg Jesus to leave their neighborhood. As he was getting into the boat, the man who had been possessed by demons begged him that he might be with him. But Jesus refused, and said to him, "Go home to your friends, and tell them how much the Lord has done for you, and what mercy he has shown you."

RESPONSE
Is there an area in your life that has been so "possessed" by demons, or addictions, so completely dominated, that only the power of God is capable of releasing their power over you?

ACTION
Today I will search for my personal demons. How do my behavior, the choices I make, and my unwillingness to tell the truth enable them to keep me enslaved?

CONCLUDING PRAYER
Generous Lord, you are ready to give us not just life, but life in abundance. Why do we prefer our commitment to foods that clog the exquisite systems of our bodies; alcohol that disintegrates our brains; greed, power, and compulsive sex that corrupt our relationships; and emotional cruelty that destroys our souls? We live in partnership with the demons we say keep us enslaved. We both know, Lord, that it is not the demons. It is us. In Jesus' name we pray. Amen.

INVITATION TO PRAYER

O Lord of generosity, you have promised to give us what
we ask for, but sometimes it feels as if our asking is not
answered. Does that mean I only have a "little faith," like
the disciples? Is the problem in what I am asking for, or how
I am asking for it, or am I looking and listening for the
answer in the wrong places? Teach me, Lord, to expand my
faith and belief in your power and goodness. Help me grow
from wanting "things" and people, and splashy miracles,
to wanting only you. Amen.

HYMN   *I Heard the Voice of Jesus Say (v. 1, 2)*

I heard the voice of Jesus say,
   "Come unto me and rest;
Lay down, O weary one, lay down
   Your head upon my breast."
I came to Jesus as I was,
   So weary, worn and sad;
I found in him a resting place,
   And he has made me glad.

I heard the voice of Jesus say,
   "Behold, I freely give
The living water, thirsty one;
   Stoop down, and drink, and live."
I came to Jesus, and I drank
   Of that life-giving stream;
My thirst was quenched, my soul revived,
   And now I live in him.

Your word is a lamp to my feet
  and a light to my path.

PSALM *Psalm 119:105, 114, 116, 130, 132, 149*
Your word is a lamp to my feet
  and a light to my path.…

You are my hiding place and my shield;
  I hope in your word.…
Uphold me according to your promise, that I might live,
  and let me not be put to shame in my hope.…

The unfolding of your words gives light;
  it imparts understanding to the simple.…
Turn to me and be gracious to me,
  as is your custom toward those who love your name.…

In your steadfast love hear my voice;
  O LORD, in your justice preserve my life.

PRAYER TO CARRY WITH ME *Psalm 119:105*
Your word is a lamp to my feet
  and a light to my path.

READING *Matthew 17:14–21*
When they came to the crowd, a man came to [Jesus], knelt
before him, and said, "Lord, have mercy on my son, for he is
an epileptic and he suffers terribly; he often falls into the fire
and often into water. And I brought him to your disciples,
but they could not cure him." Jesus answered, "You faithless
and perverse generation, how much longer must I be with
you? How much longer must I put up with you? Bring him
here to me." And Jesus rebuked the demon and it came out

of him, and the boy was cured instantly. Then the disciples came to Jesus privately and said, "Why could we not cast it out?" He said to them, "Because of your little faith. For truly I tell you, if you have faith the size of a mustard seed, you will say to this mountain, 'Move from here to there,' and it will move; and nothing will be impossible for you."

RESPONSE   *Psalm 55:22*

Cast your burden on the LORD
    and he will sustain you;
he will never permit
    the righteous to be moved.

Moved where? Moved away from our protection at his side.

ACTION

Today I will search for my personal demons. How do my behavior, the choices I make, and my unwillingness to tell the truth enable them to keep me enslaved?

CONCLUDING PRAYER

Lord Jesus, you freed the captives of blindness, leprosy, epilepsy, and possession by demons. We should not need any more miracles to prove that you are God. And yet we always ask for more. Help our infant faith grow to the size of the mustard seed, so that in your name, we can move mountains, and get well. Amen.

INVITATION TO PRAYER

O God of healing power, we are entangled with demons, some of our own making, some not. We are caught in the spiritual bondage of cruelty and greed, failure of our weak faith, loss of hope, and abandonment of our relationship with you. We have been too casual with your invitation to a whole and holy life. Please invite me again, Lord. This time my answer will be yes. In Jesus' name. Amen.

HYMN   *Eternal Spirit of the Living Christ*

Eternal Spirit of the Living Christ, I know not how to
Ask or what to say; I only know my need, as deep as life,
And only you can teach me how to pray.

Come, pray in me the prayer I need this day;
    Help me to see your
Purpose and your will,
    Where I have failed, what I have done amiss;
Held in forgiving love, let me be still.

Come with the strength I lack, bring vision clear
    Of human need; oh,
Give me eyes to see Fulfillment of my life in love outpoured:
My life in you, O Christ; your love in me. Amen.

SILENT REFLECTION ON THE DAY AND ON OURSELVES

…he sent out his word and healed them.…

PSALM *Psalm 107:1–3, 17–22*

O give thanks to the LORD, for he is good;
   for his steadfast love endures forever.
Let the redeemed of the LORD say so,
   those he redeemed from trouble
and gathered in from the lands,
   from the east and from the west,
   from the north and from the south.…

Some were sick through their sinful ways,
   and because of their iniquities endured affliction;
they loathed any kind of food,
   and they drew near to the gates of death.
Then they cried to the LORD in their trouble,
   and he saved them from their distress;
he sent out his word and healed them,
   and delivered them from destruction.
Let them thank the LORD for his steadfast love,
   or his wonderful works to humankind.
And let them offer thanksgiving sacrifices,
   and tell of his deeds with songs of joy.

PRAYER TO CARRY WITH ME *Psalm 107:20*

…he sent out his word and healed him.…

READING *Matthew 8:5–13*

When [Jesus] entered Capernaum, a centurion came to him, appealing to him and saying, "Lord, my servant is lying at home paralyzed, in terrible distress." And [Jesus] said to him, "I will come and cure him." The centurion answered,

"Lord, I am not worthy to have you come under my roof [Jewish law declared unclean any Jew who entered the house of a Gentile]; but only speak the word, and my servant will be healed. For I also am a man under authority, with soldiers under me; and I say to one, 'Go,' and he goes, and to another, 'Come,' and he comes, and to my slave, 'Do this,' and the slave does it." When Jesus heard him, he was amazed and said to those who followed him, "Truly I tell you, in no one in Israel have I found such faith. I tell you, many will come from east and west and will eat with Abraham and Isaac and Jacob in the kingdom of heaven, while the heirs of the kingdom will be thrown into the outer darkness, where there will be weeping and gnashing of teeth." And to the centurion Jesus said, "Go; let it be done for you according to your faith." And the servant was healed in that hour.

RESPONSE   *Mark 15:33–34, 37–39*

When it was noon, darkness came over the whole land until three in the afternoon. At three o'clock Jesus cried out with a loud voice, "Eloi, Eloi, lema sabachthani?" which means, "My God, my God, why have you forsaken me?"…Then Jesus gave a loud cry and breathed his last. And the curtain of the temple was torn in two, from top to bottom. Now when the centurion, who stood facing him, saw that in this way he breathed his last, he said, "Truly this man was God's Son!"

SILENT PRAYER FOR THE WORLD, OTHERS, AND OURSELVES

ACTION

Today I have searched for my personal demons. I have asked myself how my behavior, the choices I make, and my unwillingness to tell the truth enable them to keep me enslaved.

Generous Lord, you know what I need before I even ask, but I cannot always see it because I am blinded by the temptations of this world, and exhausted from chasing after them. Help me to recognize the true from the false, and to honor you in all of my choices. Amen.

STATION 11 ~ *Jesus nailed to the cross*

ADDICTION ISSUES ~ *Pain, grief, trust*

 MORNING PRAYER

INVITATION TO PRAYER

O Lord, open my lips and my mouth will declare your praise. Cleanse my heart of any worthless, evil, or distracting thoughts. Give me the energy and focus to pray with attention, and to keep our conversation going throughout this day. Let me listen more than I talk. Remind me, often, what pleases you. I can't seem to remember. Amen.

HYMN   *O Son of God, in Galilee (v. 1, 2, 4)*

O Son of God, in Galilee
   You made the deaf to hear,
The mute to speak, the blind to see;
   O blessed Lord be near.

Oh, listen to the silent prayer
   Of your afflicted ones.
Oh, bid them cast on you their care;
   Your grace to them make known.

Meanwhile to them the listening ear
   Of steadfast faith impart,
And let your word bring light and cheer
   To every troubled heart.

ANTIPHON   *Psalm 40:13*

O, LORD, make haste to help me.

PSALM

For evils have encompassed me
    without number;
my iniquities have overtaken me,
    until I cannot see;
they are more than the hairs of my head,
    and my heart fails me.

Be pleased, O LORD, to deliver me;
    O LORD, make haste to help me.
Let all those [addictive substances, destructive behaviors,
      and the people who judge me because I struggle
      with them] be put to shame and confusion
    who seek to snatch away my life;
let those be turned back and brought to dishonor
    who desire my hurt.
Let those be appalled because of their shame
    who say to me, "Aha, Aha!"

PRAYER TO CARRY WITH ME

O, LORD, make haste to help me.

READING

Once, when he was in one of the cities, there was a man covered with leprosy. When he saw Jesus, he bowed with his face to the ground and begged him, "Lord, if you choose, you can make me clean." Then Jesus stretched out his hand, touched him, and said, "I do choose. Be made clean." Immediately the leprosy left him. And he ordered him to tell no one. "Go," he said, "and show yourself to the priest, and, as Moses commanded, make an offering for your cleansing.…" [T]he word about Jesus spread abroad; many crowds would gather to hear him and to be cured of their diseases. But he would withdraw to deserted places and pray.

RESPONSE
Jesus asks, "Do you want to get well?" Do I? What will I gain, and what will I lose? Maybe I will have to give up things I'm not ready to give up. Maybe I don't have anything else yet to fill the space in my life that my addiction occupies. For me, is the cure worse than the disease? Do I *really* want to get well?

ACTION
Today, whenever I am tempted to choose what is toxic to me, I will say, as Jesus did: "I do choose." Let me "be made clean."

CONCLUDING PRAYER
Breathe on me, breath of God,
fill me with life anew,
That I may love the things you love,
And do what you would do.
Amen.

 MIDDAY PRAYER

INVITATION TO PRAYER
O patient Lord, it is noontime and I am in the midst of my busy life. Help me to make choices that are life-giving, and to stay on guard against destructive activities, substances, or relationships. I know you want my body to be clean and fit, but I also know that cannot happen until my spirit begins to heal. Help me practice this new skill. I'm not very good at it yet. In Jesus' name. Amen.

Lord, save your world; in bitter need
To you your children raise their plea;
We wait your liberating deed
To signal hope and set us free.

Lord, save your world; our souls are bound
In iron chains of fear and pride;
High walls of ignorance abound
And faces from each other hide.

Lord, save your world; we strive in vain
To save ourselves without your aid;
What skill and science slowly gain
Is seen to evil ends betrayed.

Lord, save your world, since you have sent
The Savior whom we sorely need;
For us his tears and blood were spent
That from our bonds we might be freed.

ANTIPHON   *Psalm 106:36*

They served their idols,
   which became a snare to them.

PSALM   *Psalm 106:34–39*

[The Israelites] did not destroy the [pagan] peoples,
   as the LORD commanded them,
but they mingled with the nations
   and learned to do as they did.

They served their idols,
    which became a snare to them.
They sacrificed their sons
    and their daughters to the demons;
they poured out innocent blood,
    the blood of their sons and daughters,
whom they sacrificed to the idols….;
    and the land was polluted with blood.
Thus they became unclean by their acts,
    and prostituted themselves in their doings.

PRAYER TO CARRY WITH ME *Psalm 106:36*
They served their idols,
    which became a snare to them.

READING *Deuteronomy 32:16–17*
[God's chosen people] made him jealous with strange gods,
    with abhorrent things they provoked him.
[The people] sacrificed to demons, not God,
    to deities they had never known,
    to new ones recently arrived,
        whom [their] ancestors had not feared.

RESPONSE *Joshua 24:15*
"Now if you are unwilling to serve the LORD, choose this day
whom you will serve, whether the [pagan] gods your ancestors served…or the gods…in whose land you are living; but
as for me and my household, we will serve the LORD."

ACTION
Today, when I am tempted by what is toxic for me, I will
choose not to "serve my idols" or let them be a "snare" to
me. I have a choice. I *always* have a choice.

I love the LORD, because he has heard
   my voice and my supplications.
Because he inclined his ear to me,
   therefore I will call on him as long as I live.
Amen.

 EVENING PRAYER

INVITATION TO PRAYER

O, God of Love, your beautiful world, the one you gave us,
is tearing itself apart. Everywhere there is violence; we are
saturated with it. We are violent when we claw and scratch
one another to get an advantage, or criticize someone to
make ourselves feel "better." Especially now, at the end of
the day, it is so tempting to eat or drink or smoke something
to soothe our wounded spirits and bodies. Help us to
remember that our only true and lasting relief is in you.
Amen.

HYMN   *A New Commandment*

Refrain
I give you a new commandment:
Love one another as I have loved
you, as I have loved you.

This is my will, my one command,
That love should dwell among you all.
This is my will, that you should love
As I have shown that I love you.

Refrain

You chose not me, but I chose you,
That you should go and bear much fruit.
I chose you out that you in me
Should bear much fruit that will abide.

Refrain

All that you ask my Father dear
For my name's sake you shall receive.
This is my will, my one command,
That love should dwell in each, in all.

Refrain

ANTIPHON
Psalm 66:20

Blessed be God,
> because he has not rejected my prayer
> or removed his steadfast love from me.

PSALM
Psalm 66:8–12

Bless our God, O peoples,
> let the sound of his praise be heard,
who has kept us among the living,
> and has not let our feet slip.
For you, O God, have tested us;
> you have tried us as silver is tried.
You brought us into the net;
> you laid burdens on our backs;
you let people ride over our heads;
> we went through fire and through water;
yet you have brought us out to a spacious place.

PRAYER TO CARRY WITH ME
Psalm 66:20

Blessed be God,
> because he has not rejected my prayer
> or removed his steadfast love from me.

READING
Luke 17:11–19

On the way to Jerusalem Jesus was going through the region between Samaria and Galilee. As he entered a village, ten lepers approached him. Keeping their distance, they called out, saying, "Jesus, Master, have mercy on us!" When he saw them, he said to them, "Go and show yourselves to the priests." And as they went, they were made clean. Then one of them, when he saw that he was healed, turned back, praising God with a loud voice. He prostrated himself at Jesus' feet and thanked him. And he was a Samaritan. Then Jesus asked, "Were not ten made clean? But the other nine, where are they? Was none of them found to return and give praise to God except this foreigner?" Then he said to him, "Get up and go on your way; your faith has made you well."

RESPONSE
Matthew 12:34

....out of the abundance of the heart the mouth speaks.

ACTION
Today, whenever I am tempted to choose what is toxic to me, I will say, as Jesus did: "I do choose. Be made clean." When my heart is overflowing with gratitude, I can begin to make that choice.

CONCLUDING PRAYER
Our generous God, thank you for this day. Please quiet our racing minds, and calm our tense and tired bodies. May your help always renew us and keep us strong in this hard

work of healing to which we have committed ourselves. It would be unthinkable without the strength of your presence and your steadfast love. And now, send peaceful sleep to refresh us for tomorrow. In Jesus' name. Amen.

 ## NIGHT PRAYER

INVITATION TO PRAYER

O God of quiet, at the end of this day, let me relax into you and let go of all the weariness and the worrying I have accumulated today. It is a paradox that I can expend so much effort and energy on other peoples' lives, and yet be so self-centered. Wherever I go, I drag the consequences of my addiction with me. I feel awkward, ashamed, guilty, as if people whisper behind my back about what a loser I am. And I am a loser, because I'm losing out on your best gift: my life. Can you help me find a better way to live than dividing my time between thinking about doing my addiction and thinking about how shamed I feel. I have abandoned myself. Lord Jesus, please don't abandon me. Amen.

HYMN   *If You but Trust in God to Guide You*

If you but trust in God to guide you
And place your confidence in him,
You'll find him always there beside you,
To give you hope and strength within.
For those who trust God's changeless love,
Built on the rock that will not move.

What gain is there in futile weeping,
In helpless anger and distress?
If you are in his care and keeping,

In sorrow will he love you less?
For he who took for you a cross
Will bring you safe through every loss.

SILENT REFLECTION ON THE DAY AND ON OURSELVES

ANTIPHON   *Psalm 91:11*

For he will command his angels concerning you
    to guard you in all your ways.

PSALM   *Psalm 91:14–16b*

Those who love me, I will deliver;
    I will protect those who know my name.
When they call to me, I will answer them;
    I will be with them in trouble,
    I will rescue them and honor them.…
    and show them my salvation.

PRAYER TO CARRY WITH ME   *Psalm 91:11*

For he will command his angels concerning you
    to guard you in all your ways.

READING   *Luke 4:1–4, 9–13*

Jesus, full of the Holy Spirit, returned from the Jordan and
was led by the Spirit in the wilderness, where for forty days
he was tempted by the devil. He ate nothing at all during
those days, and when they were over, he was famished.
The devil said to him, "If you are the Son of God, command
this stone to become a loaf of bread." Jesus answered him,
"It is written, 'One does not live by bread alone.'…"

Then the devil took him to Jerusalem, and placed him on
the pinnacle of the temple, saying to him, "If you are the Son
of God, throw yourself down from here, for it is written,

'He will command his angels concerning you,
to protect you,'

and

'On their hands they will bear you up,
so that you will not dash your foot
against a stone.'"

Jesus answered him, "It is said, 'Do not put the Lord your
God to the test.'" When the devil had finished every test,
he departed from him until an opportune time.

RESPONSE
1 Peter 5:8

Discipline yourselves. Keep alert. Like a roaring lion your
adversary the devil prowls around, looking for someone
to devour.

SILENT PRAYER FOR THE WORLD, OTHERS, AND OURSELVES

ACTION
Today, whenever I was tempted to choose what is toxic
to me, I said, as Jesus did: "I do choose. Be made clean."
It was very hard.

CONCLUDING PRAYER
*Briefly It Enters,
and Briefly Speaks*

I am the blossom pressed in a book,
found again after two hundred years....

I am the maker, the lover, and the keeper....

When the young girl who starves
sits down to a table
she will sit beside me....

I am food on the prisoner's plate....

I am water rushing to the well-head,
filling the pitcher until it spills....

I am the patient gardener
of the dry and weedy garden...

I am the stone step,
the latch, and the working hinge....

I am the heart contracted by joy...
the longest hair, white
before the rest....

I am there in the basket of fruit
presented to the widow....

I am the musk rose opening
unattended, the fern on the boggy summit....

I am the one whose love
overcomes you, already with you
when you think to call my name....

JANE KENYON

STATION 12 ~ *Jesus dies on the cross*

ADDICTION ISSUES ~ *Belief, relapse, deliverance*

 MORNING PRAYER

INVITATION TO PRAYER

O Lord, open my eyes to see your gracious hand in all your
works. Be present this morning and give to us, those who
love you, the peace that cannot come from the world,
so that we can set our hearts to obey your commandments.
Defend us from our enemies so that we may live in peace,
in quietness, and in gratitude for the lives you have given us.
In Jesus' name. Amen.

HYMN   *You Are Mine (David Haas)*

I will come to you in the silence,
I will lift you from all your fear.
You will hear my voice, I claim you as my choice,
be still and know that I am here.

Refrain
Do not be afraid, I am with you.
I have called you each by name.
Come and follow, I will bring you home;
I love you and you are mine.

I am hope for all who are hopeless,
I am eyes for all who long to see.
In the shadows of the night, I will be your light,
come and rest in me.

I am strength for all the despairing,
healing for the ones who dwell in shame.
All the blind will see, the lame will all run free,
and all will know my name.

Refrain

I am the Word that leads all to freedom
I am the peace the world cannot give.
I will call your name, embracing all your pain,
stand up, now walk, and live!

Refrain

ANTIPHON   *You Are Mine (v. 3)*

I am strength for…the despairing,
healing for [all] who dwell in shame.

PSALM   *Psalm 19:9–14*

[T]he fear of the LORD is pure,
    enduring forever;
the ordinances of the LORD are true
    and righteous altogether.
More to be desired are they than gold,
    even much fine gold;
sweeter also than honey,
    and drippings of the honeycomb.

Moreover by them is your servant warned;
    in keeping them there is great reward.
But who can detect their errors?
    Clear me from hidden faults.

Keep back your servant also from the insolent;
   do not let them have dominion over me.
Then I shall be [whole,]
   and innocent of great transgression.

Let the words of my mouth and the meditation of my heart
   be acceptable to you,
   O LORD, my rock and my redeemer.

PRAYER TO CARRY WITH ME   *You Are Mine (v. 3)*
I am strength for… the despairing,
healing for [all] who dwell in shame.

READING   *Matthew 13:3–9*
[Jesus] told [the people] many things in parables, saying:
"Listen! A sower went out to sow. And as he sowed, some
seeds fell on the path, and the birds came and ate them up.
Other seeds fell on rocky ground, where they did not have
much soil, and they sprang up quickly.…But when the sun
rose, they were scorched; and since they had no root, they
withered away. Other seeds fell among thorns, and the
thorns grew up and choked them. Other seeds fell on good
soil and brought forth grain, some a hundredfold, some
sixty, some thirty. Let anyone with ears listen!"

RESPONSE   *Matthew 13:13–16, 18–24*
"The reason I speak to [the people] in parables is that
'seeing they do not perceive, and hearing they do not listen,
nor do they understand.…'

   '…with their heart[s] and turn—
      and I would heal them.'

"Hear then the parable of the sower. When anyone hears the word of the kingdom and does not understand it, the evil one comes and snatches away what is sown in the heart; this is what was sown…on the path. As for what was sown on rocky ground, this is the one who hears the word and immediately receives it with joy; yet such a person has no root, but endures only for a while, and when trouble or persecution arises that person immediately falls away. As for what was sown among thorns, this is the one who hears the word, but the cares of the world and the lure of wealth choke the word, and it yields nothing. But as for what was sown on good soil, this is the one who hears the word and understands it, who indeed bears fruit and yields, in one case a hundredfold, in another sixty, and in another thirty."

ACTION

Can you identify with the seed that "was sown on rocky ground"? The one that hears God's word and "receives it with joy," but that "endures only for a while"…[until] "trouble or persecution arises, [and then it] immediately falls away"?

Today I will identify one new situation or relationship, or one gift God that has already given me, that can "fertilize" my fragile root so it will become strong, and I will be able to cling to my Rock without fear.

We forget, and need reminding, that each day "breaks" upon us as an offering from God to begin anew, to re-energize our hopes, to become more fully "in His image." A "pulse" beats over and over, signifying life. Every repetition only carries us forward:

Lift up your eyes
Upon this day breaking for you.
Give birth again
To the dream.

Women, children, men,
Take it into the palms of your hands,
Mold it into the shape of your most
Private need. Sculpt it into
The image of your most public self.
Lift up your hearts
Each new hour holds new chances
For a new beginning.
Do not be wedded forever
To fear, yoked eternally
To brutishness.

The horizon leans forward,
Offering you space
To place new steps of change
Here, on the pulse of this fine day
You may have courage
To look up and out and upon me,
The Rock, the River, the Tree, your country.

No less to Midas than to the mendicant.
No less to you now than the mastodon then.

Here on the pulse of this new day
You may have the grace to look up and out
And into your sister's eyes,
And into your brother's face,
Your country,
And say simply
Very simply
With hope—
Good morning.

MAYA ANGELOU

 MIDDAY PRAYER

INVITATION TO PRAYER

O faithful God, despite my best efforts, I slip, lose my
footing, and fall back into the slavery of my old habits and
relationships. Just when I think I have put self-destructive
behavior behind me, I am swallowed up again by unrelent-
ing cravings. You have promised to those who love you that
you will shield and protect us from temptations; maybe I
don't understand what that really means, or how it works.
Please show me, again. Amen

HYMN   *Who Trusts in God, a Strong Abode*

Who trusts in God, a strong abode
   In heaven and earth possesses;
Who looks in love to Christ above,
   No fear that heart oppresses.

In you alone, dear Lord, we own
     Sweet hope and consolation,
Our shield from foes, our balm for woes,
     our great and sure salvation.

Though Satan's wrath beset our path
     And worldly scorn assail us,
While you are near, we shall not fear;
     Your strength will never fail us.

Your rod and staff will keep us safe
And guide our steps forever;
     Nor shades of death nor hell beneath,
Our lives from you will sever.

ANTIPHON
While you are near, we shall not fear;
Your strength will never fail us.

PSALM   *Psalm 18:1–2, 6, 16–17, 19, 31–33, 36–38, 42, 46*
I love you, O LORD, my strength.
The LORD is my rock, my fortress, and my deliverer,
     my God, my rock in whom I take refuge,
     my shield, and the horn of my salvation,
          my stronghold.…

In my distress I called upon the LORD;
     to my God I cried for help.
From his temple he heard my voice,
     and my cry to him reached his ears.…

He reached down from on high, he took me;
     he drew me out of mighty waters.

He delivered me from my strong enem[ies]
    [addictive substances and behaviors],…
    for they were too mighty for me.…
He brought me out into a broad place;
    he delivered me, because he delighted in me.

For who is God except the LORD?
    And who is a rock besides our God?—
the God who girded me with strength,
    and made my way safe.
He made my feet like the feet of a deer,
    and set me secure on the heights.…
You gave me a wide place for my steps under me,
    and my feet did not slip.
I pursued my enemies [addictive substances and behaviors]
      and overtook them.…
I struck them [addictive substances and behaviors] down,
    so that they were not able to rise;
    they fell under my feet.…
I beat them fine, like dust before the wind;
    I cast them out like the mire of the streets.

The LORD lives! Blessed be my rock,
    and exalted be the God of my salvation.

PRAYER TO CARRY WITH ME
While you are near, we shall not fear;
Your strength will never fail us.

READING   *Matthew 7:24–27*

"Everyone then who hears these words of mine and acts on
them will be like a wise man who built his house on rock.
The rain fell, the floods came, and the winds blew and beat
on that house, but it did not fall, because it had been founded on rock. And everyone who hears these words of mine
and does not act on them will be like a foolish man who built
his house on sand. The rain fell, and the floods came, and
the winds blew and beat against that house, and it fell—and
great was its fall!"

RESPONSE   *1 Corinthians 6:17, 19–20*

…anyone united to the Lord becomes one spirit with
him.…[D]o you not know that your body is a temple of the
Holy Spirit within you, which you have from God, and that
you are not your own? For you were bought with a price;
therefore [honor] God [with] your body.

ACTION

Today I will identify one new situation or relationship,
or one gift God has already given me, that can strengthen
my foundation so and I will be able to withstand whatever
tries to tear me down.

CONCLUDING PRAYER

O God, source of all strength, uphold me when I am weak,
send light for your path when I am lost, send clarity of mind
when I am confused, send your peace when I am willful.
Bring your stabilizing hand into my life when I lose my
direction and wander, or run, toward my addictions, those
artificial pleasures that can never compare with your love
for me. In Jesus' name. Amen.

INVITATION TO PRAYER

O Lord, we are like the Israelites who fell into captivity again after you had freed them from slavery in Egypt. They were taken to Babylon against their will, and forced to labor for their captors. I am, as they were, back in chains for foolishly thinking your promise of abundant life could come by living free from your commandments. Lord, forgive in me the arrogance to think I can maintain old habits and relationships that undermine my commitment to live in your light and walk in your path. In Jesus' name. Amen.

HYMN   *By the Babylonian Rivers*

By the Babylonian rivers
   we sat down in grief and wept;
hung our harps up on a willow,
   mourned for Zion when we slept.

There our captors in derision
   did require of us a song;
so we sat with staring vision,
   and the days were long and hard.

How shall we sing the Lord's song
   in a strange and bitter land?
Can our voices veil the sorrow?
   Lord God, hold your holy band.

Let the cross be benediction
   for those bound in tyranny;
by the power of resurrection
   loose them from captivity.

ANTIPHON
Let the cross be benediction for those bound in tyranny....

PSALM   *Psalm 6:1–2, 4, 6–9*
O LORD, do not rebuke me in your anger,
  or discipline me in your wrath.
Be gracious to me, O LORD, for I am languishing;
  O LORD, heal me, for my bones are shaking with terror....

Turn, O LORD, save my life;
  deliver me for the sake of your steadfast love....

I am weary with my moaning;
  every night I flood my bed with tears;
  I drench my couch with my weeping.
My eyes waste away because of grief;
  they grow weak because of all my foes
  [addictive substances and behaviors].

Depart from me, all you workers of evil
  [addictive substances and behaviors],
  for the LORD has heard the sound of my weeping.
The LORD has heard my supplication;
  the LORD accepts my prayer.

PRAYER TO CARRY WITH ME
...by the power of resurrection loose [us] from captivity.

READING   *Luke 11:20–28*
[Jesus said] "...if it is by the finger of God that I cast out the
demons, then the kingdom of God has come to you....

  "When the unclean spirit has gone out of a person, it
wanders through waterless regions looking for a resting
place, but not finding any, it says, 'I will return to my house

from which I came.' When it comes, it finds it swept and put in order. Then it goes and brings seven other spirits more evil than itself, and they enter and live there; and the last state of that person is worse than the first."

While he was saying this, a woman in the crowd raised her voice and said to him, "Blessed is the [mother who gave you birth and] nursed you!" But he said, "Blessed rather are those who hear the word of God and obey it!"

RESPONSE   *Matthew 9:17*

"Neither is new wine put into old wineskins; otherwise, the skins burst, and the wine is spilled, and the skins are destroyed; but new wine is put into fresh wineskins, and so both are preserved."

We cannot banish our demons and then leave a vacant space where they once lived in our mind and body. We have to fill the emptiness with "new wine," with new foods, friends, or activities, and with gifts God has already given us that we overlooked in our addictive obsession. Then there will be no home for the demon when it returns (and it will), bringing others with it.

ACTION

Have you ever lost ten pounds, and in the course of celebrating that victory been careless and gained back twenty?

Today I will identify one new situation or relationship, or one gift God has already given me that will remind and help me to fill the empty space left behind when the demon is banished.

Let the light of late afternoon
shine through chinks in the barn, moving
up the bales as the sun moves down.

Let the cricket take up chafing
as a women takes up her needles
and her yarn. Let evening come.

Let dew collect on the hoe abandoned
in long grass. Let the stars appear
and the moon disclose her silver horn.

Let the fox go back to its shady den.
Let the wind die down. Let the shed
go black inside. Let evening come.

To the bottle in the ditch, to the scoop
in the oats, to air in the lung
let evening come.

Let it come, as it will, and don't
be afraid. God does not leave us
comfortless, so let evening come.

JANE KENYON

 NIGHT PRAYER

INVITATION TO PRAYER

O Lord, I try to follow you, but I trip in the dark and lose my way. Help me to let go of my self-deception and rationalization. They do not light my path. There is *no* circumstance where my addictions will protect me better than you do.

Show me your path Lord, in a way I can understand, and then please, come back and get me. Amen.

HYMN   *"Come Follow Me," the Savior Spake (v. 1, 2, 4)*

"Come follow me." The Savior spake,
   "All in my way abiding;
Deny yourselves the world forsake,
   Obey my call and guiding.
O bear the cross, whate'er betide;
   Take my example for your guide."

"I am the light; I light the way,
   A godly life displaying;
I bid you walk as in the day;
   I keep your feet from straying.
I am the way, and well I show
   How you should sojourn here below."

"I teach you how to shun and flee
   What harms your soul's salvation;
Your heart from every guile to free,
   From sin and its temptation.
I am the refuge of the soul
   And lead you to your heavenly goal."

**SILENT REFLECTION ON THE DAY
AND ON OURSELVES**

ANTIPHON

"I teach you how to shun and flee
What harms your soul's salvation."

PSALM

O L̲ord, our Sovereign,
   how majestic is your name in all the earth!

You have set your glory above the heavens.
   Out of the mouths of babes and infants
you have founded a bulwark because of your foes,
   to silence the enemy and the avenger.

When I look at your heavens, the work of your fingers,
   the moon and the stars that you have [set in place];
what are human beings that you are mindful of them,
   mortals that you care for them?

Yet you have made them a little lower than God,
   and crowned them with glory and honor.
You have given them dominion over the works
      of your hands;
   you have put all things under their feet,
all sheep and oxen,
   and also the beasts of the field,
the birds of the air, and the fish of the sea,
   [all that swim] the paths of the seas.

O L̲ord, our Sovereign,
   how majestic is your name in all the earth!

PRAYER TO CARRY WITH ME
"I teach you how to shun and flee
What harms your soul's salvation."

READING
Romans 7:15–25

I do not understand my own actions. For I do not do what I want, but I do the very thing I hate.…I can will what is right, but I cannot do it. For I do not do the good I want, but the evil I do not want is what I do.…

So I find it to be a law that when I want to do what is good, evil lies close at hand.…Wretched man that I am! Who will rescue me from this body of death? Thanks be to God through Jesus Christ our Lord!

RESPONSE
Matthew 6:24

"No one can serve two masters; for [he] will either hate the one and love the other, or be devoted to the one and despise the other." We cannot serve God and [addictions].

SILENT PRAYER FOR THE WORLD, OTHERS, AND OURSELVES

ACTION
Today I have identified one new situation, relationship, or gift God has already given me that will help me resolve the war going on inside me, where I keep switching sides. Lord, help me always to prefer you. Amen.

CONCLUDING PRAYER
The Liturgy of the Hours

Protect us, Lord, as we stay awake;
   watch over us as we sleep, that awake,
we may keep watch with Christ,
   and asleep, rest in his peace. Amen.

STATION 13 ~ *Jesus' body taken down from the cross*

ADDICTION ISSUES ~ *Despair, loss, death*

 ## MORNING PRAYER

INVITATION TO PRAYER

O Lord, open my lips, my eyes, my ears, and my heart
so I can say, "Yes" to your invitation. Cleanse my heart of
anything that distracts my attention. Give me the patience
and love to pray carefully, so that I can hear your voice.
I have used my addiction to fill up my emptiness; now I
understand it is you I crave. Now I will fill my loneliness
with prayer; mostly, I will listen. Amen.

HYMN   *Rise, My Soul, to Watch and Pray*

Rise my soul, to watch and pray;
   From your sleep awaken;
Be not by the evil day
   Unawares o'er taken. Satan's prey oft are they
Who secure are sleeping
   And no watch are keeping.

Watch against the world that frowns
   Darkly to dismay you;
Watch when it your wishes crowns;
   Smiling to betray you. Watch and see, you are free
From false friends who charm you
   While they seek to harm you.

Watch against yourself, my soul,
    Lest with grace you trifle;
Let not self your thoughts control
    Nor God's mercy stifle. Pride and sin lurk within,
All your hopes to shatter;
    Heed not when they flatter.

But while watching, also pray
    To the Lord unceasing.
God alone can make you free,
    Strength and faith increasing, So that still mind and will
Heartfelt praises tender
    And true service render.

ANTIPHON

Psalm 22:8

"Commit your cause to the LORD...
    let him rescue the one in whom he delights!"

PSALM

Psalm 22:1–8 (traditionally chanted during the Triduum)

My God, my God, why have you forsaken me?
    Why are you so far from helping me,
        from the words of my groaning?
O my God, I cry by day, but you do not answer;
    and by night, but find no rest.

Yet you are holy,
    enthroned on the praises of Israel.
In you our ancestors trusted;
    they trusted, and you delivered them.
To you they cried, and were saved;
    in you they trusted, and were not put to shame.

But I am a worm, and not human;
    scorned by others, and despised by the people.
All who see me mock at me;
    they make mouths at me, they shake their heads;
"Commit your cause to the LORD; let him deliver—
    let him rescue the one in whom he delights!"

PRAYER TO CARRY WITH ME   *Psalm 22:8*
"Commit your cause to the LORD…
    let him rescue the one in whom he delights!"

READING   *Matthew 26:36–41*
Then Jesus went with them to a place called Gethsemane;
and he said to his disciples, "Sit here while I go over there
and pray"…and [he] began to be grieved and agitated. Then
he said to them, "I am deeply grieved, even to death; remain
here, and stay awake with me." And going a little farther, he
threw himself on the ground and prayed, "My Father, if it is
possible, let this cup pass from me; yet not what I want but
what you want." Then he came to the disciples and found
them sleeping; and he said to Peter, "So, could you not stay
awake with me one hour? Stay awake and pray that you may
not come into the time of trial; the spirit indeed is willing,
but the flesh is weak."

RESPONSE
Am I like Peter? When Christ calls me to an intimate
relationship with him, do I go to sleep? Do the cravings
of my "weak flesh" overcome my spirit? Do I lose myself
in the fog of the addiction that cannot be healed,
until I can say with conviction and joy, "Here I am Lord"?

ACTION

Today I will try to see and feel the difference between
my will and God's will.

CONCLUDING PRAYER

Lord, make me an instrument of your peace:
Where there is hatred, let me sow love;
Where there is injury, pardon;
Where there is doubt, faith;
Where there is despair, hope;
Where there is darkness, light;
Where there is sadness, joy;
Lord, may I not so much seek
To be consoled as to console;
To be understood as to understand;
To be loved as to love.
Because it is in giving that we receive,
In pardoning that we are pardoned. Amen.

 MIDDAY PRAYER

INVITATION TO PRAYER

O Holy God, we can cause terrible damage to those we love
and to ourselves when we become entangled in the tentacles
of addiction. Help me to cast off deadly attitudes, behaviors,
and toxins. I am scared, Lord, to live my life without the
addictions I've used to support me. I know I can walk without them, but only with your hand leading me and your
strong arm supporting me. I love you. Amen.

Be Not Afraid (Robert J. Dufford, SJ)

You shall cross the barren desert,
  but you shall not die of thirst.
You shall wander far in safety
  though you do not know the way.
You shall speak your words in foreign lands
  and all will understand.
You shall see the face of God and live.

Refrain
Be not afraid. I go before you always
Come, follow me, and I will give you rest.

If you pass through raging waters in the sea,
  you shall not drown.
If you walk amid the burning flames,
  you shall not be harmed.
If you stand before the power of hell
  and death is at your side,
know that I am with you through it all.

Refrain

Blessed are your poor,
  for the kingdom shall be theirs.
Blest are you that weep and mourn,
  for one day you shall laugh.
And if wicked tongues insult and hate you
  all because of me,
Blessed, blessed are you.

Refrain

Blest are you that weep and mourn,
   for one day you shall laugh.

PSALM *Psalm 22:9–17*

Yet it was you who took me from the womb;
   you kept me safe on my mother's breast.
On you I was cast from my birth,
   and since my mother bore me you have been my God.
Do not be far from me,
   for trouble is near and there is no one to help.

Many bulls encircle me,
   strong bulls of Bashan surround me;
they open wide their mouths at me,
   like a ravening and roaring lion.

I am poured out like water,
   and all my bones are out of joint;
my heart is like wax;
   it is melted within my breast;
my mouth is dried up like a potsherd,
   and my tongue sticks to my jaws;
     you lay me in the dust of death.

For dogs are all around me;
   a company of evildoers encircles me.
My hands and feet have shriveled;
I can count all my bones.
They stare and gloat over me.

Blest are you who weep and mourn,
   for one day you shall laugh.

READING   *Matthew 5:3–12*

"Blessed are the poor in spirit, for theirs is the kingdom of heaven.

"Blessed are those who mourn, for they will be comforted.

"Blessed are the meek, for they will inherit the earth."

"Blessed are those who hunger and thirst for righteousness, for they will be filled.

"Blessed are the merciful, for they will receive mercy.

"Blessed are the pure in heart, for they will see God.

"Blessed are the peacemakers, for they will be called children of God.

"Blessed are those who are persecuted for righteousness' sake, for theirs is the kingdom of heaven.

"Blessed are you when people revile you and persecute you and utter all kinds of evil against you falsely on my account. Rejoice and be glad, for your reward is great in heaven, for in the same way they persecuted the prophets who were before you."

RESPONSE   *Matthew 6:20–21*

"…store up for yourselves treasures in heaven, where neither moth nor rust consumes and where thieves do not break in and steal. For where your treasure is, there your heart will be also."

ACTION

Today I will try to see the difference between God's will and my will, God's economy and the world's economy.

CONCLUDING PRAYER   *Our Father*

Our Father, who art in heaven, hallowed be thy name;
thy kingdom come, thy will be done on earth
as it is in heaven.
Give us this day our daily bread; and forgive us our
trespasses, as we forgive those who trespass against us;
and lead us not into temptation, but deliver us from evil.
For the kingdom, the power, and the glory are yours
now and for ever. Amen.

Lord God, send peaceful sleep to refresh our tired bodies.
May your help always renew us and keep us strong in your
service. We ask this through Christ our Lord. Amen.

 EVENING PRAYER

INVITATION TO PRAYER

O loving Lord, you reach out to us in the guise of sinners
and saints who teach us about you. We have learned from
Mother Teresa, that "… the greatest suffering is to feel
alone, unwanted; [that…. Jesus] comes to us in the
hungry, the naked, the lonely, the alcoholic, the drug addict,
the prostitute, the street beggars. He may come to [us] in a
father who is alone, in a mother, in a brother, or in a sister,
[or in myself?]. If we reject them… we reject Jesus himself."
Come now, Lord Jesus. Amen.

HYMN   *Were You There*

Were you there when they crucified my Lord?
Were you there when they crucified my Lord? Oh, _____

Sometimes it causes me to tremble, tremble, tremble,
were you there when they crucified my Lord?

Were you there when they nailed him to the tree?
Were you there when they nailed him to the tree? Oh, _____
sometimes it causes me to tremble, tremble, tremble,
were you there when they nailed him to the tree?

Were you there when they laid him in the tomb?
Were you there when they laid him in the tomb? Oh, _____
Sometimes it causes me to tremble, tremble, tremble,
were you there when they laid him in the tomb?

ANTIPHON   *Taizé*

Jesus remember me, when you come into your kingdom.

PSALM   *Psalm 22:18–23*

…they divide my clothes among themselves,
    and for my clothing they cast lots.

But you, O LORD, do not be far away!
    O my help, come quickly to my aid!
Deliver my soul from the sword,
    my life from the power of the dog!
Save me from the mouth of the lion!
    From the horns of the wild oxen you have rescued me.
I will tell of your name to my brothers and sisters;
    in the midst of the congregation I will praise you:
You who fear the LORD, praise him!
    All you offspring of Jacob, glorify him;
    stand in awe of him, all you offspring of Israel!

PRAYER TO CARRY WITH ME   *Taizé*

Jesus remember me, when you come into your kingdom.

Luke 23:32–43; Matthew 27:45–46, 50

Two others also, who were criminals, were led away to be put to death with him. When they came to the place that is called The Skull, they crucified Jesus there with the criminals, one on his right and one on his left. Then Jesus said, "Father, forgive them; for they do not know what they are doing." And they cast lots to divide his clothing....The soldiers...mocked him, coming up and offering him sour wine, and saying, "If you are the King of the Jews, save yourself!" There was also an inscription over him, "This is the King of the Jews."

One of the criminals who were hanged there kept deriding him and saying, "Are you not the Messiah? Save yourself and us!" But the other rebuked him, saying, "Do you not fear God, since you are under the same sentence of condemnation? And we indeed have been condemned justly, for we are getting what we deserve for our deeds, but this man has done nothing wrong." Then he said, "Jesus, remember me when you come into your kingdom." He replied, "Truly I tell you, today you will be with me in Paradise."

From noon on, darkness came over the whole land until three in the afternoon. And about three o'clock Jesus cried with a loud voice, "Eli, Eli, lema sabachthani?" that is, "My God, my God, why have you forsaken me?"...Then Jesus cried again with a loud voice and breathed his last.

RESPONSE   *Mother Teresa*

True love causes pain.

Jesus, in order to give us the proof of his love,
died on a cross.

A mother, in order to give birth to her baby, has to suffer.

If you really love one another, you will not be able to avoid making sacrifices.

Jesus says, "I was sick and you took care of me."
If I sacrifice my addiction and take care of myself in my
"sickness," am I taking care of the Jesus who loves me?
Is he worthy of my love? He has already shown me that
I am worthy of his.

ACTION

Today I will remember: I'm not loved because I'm beautiful, I'm beautiful because I'm loved.

CONCLUDING PRAYER   *Prayer of Saint Ignatius*

Lord, teach me to be generous.
Teach me to serve you as you deserve;
to give without counting the cost;
to fight and not to heed the wounds;
to toil and not to seek for rest;
to labor and not to ask for reward,
except to know that I am doing your will.
Amen.

 NIGHT PRAYER

INVITATION TO PRAYER

O God of love, we thank you for bringing us safely to the end of this day. Through Christ's sacrifice you have won us for yourself. You have drawn us out of the terrible darkness he endured out of love for us, and obedience to you, and into your brilliant light. Thank you, thank you. Amen.

The Day You Gave Us, Lord, Has Ended

The day you gave us Lord, has ended;
The darkness falls at your behest.
To you our morning hymns ascending;
Your praise shall hallow now our rest.

We thank you that your Church, unsleeping
While earth rolls onward into light,
Through all the world its watch is keeping,
And never rests by day or night.

As to each continent and island
The dawn leads on another day,
The voice of prayer is never silent,
Fresh hymns of thankful praise arise.

SILENT REFLECTION ON THE DAY AND ON OURSELVES

ANTIPHON   *Psalm 22:24*

...[the LORD] did not despise or abhor
  the affliction of the afflicted....

PSALM   *Psalm 22:24–31*

For he did not despise or abhor
  the affliction of the afflicted;
he did not hide his face from me,
  but heard when I cried to him.

From you comes my praise in the great congregation;
  my vows I will pay before those who fear him.
The poor shall eat and be satisfied;
  those who seek him shall praise the LORD.
  May your hearts live forever!

All the ends of the earth shall remember
 and turn to the LORD;
and all the families of the nations
 shall worship before him.
For dominion belongs to the LORD,
 and he rules over the nations.

To him, indeed, shall all who sleep in the earth bow down;
 before him shall bow all who go down to the dust,
 and I shall live for him.
Posterity will serve him;
 future generations will be told about the LORD,
and proclaim his deliverance to a people yet unborn,
 saying that he has done it.

PRAYER TO CARRY WITH ME   *Psalm 22:24*
...[the LORD] did not despise or abhor
 the affliction of the afflicted....

READING   *Matthew 27:51–54*
At that moment the curtain of the temple was torn in two,
from top to bottom. The earth shook, and the rocks were
split. The tombs also were opened, and many bodies of the
saints who had fallen asleep were raised. After his resurrection they came out of the tombs and entered the holy city
and appeared to many. Now when the centurion and those
with him, who were keeping watch over Jesus, saw the earth-
quake and what took place, they were terrified and said,
"Truly this man was God's Son!"

O LORD, you brought up my soul from [the dead];
restored me to life from among those gone down to the Pit.

Can I claim this miracle for myself, today?

SILENT PRAYER FOR THE WORLD, OTHERS, AND OURSELVES

ACTION

Today I have tried to see and feel the difference between
my will and God's will and God's economy and the world's
economy.

CONCLUDING PRAYER   *Prayer of Confession*
and Forgiveness

Most merciful God, we confess that we are in bondage to sin
and cannot free ourselves.

We have sinned against you in thought, word, and deed,
by what we have done and by what we have left undone.
We have not loved you with our whole heart; we have not
loved our neighbors as ourselves. For the sake of your Son,
Jesus Christ, have mercy on us. Forgive us, renew us, and
lead us, so that we may delight in your will and walk in your
ways, to the glory of your holy name. Amen.

STATION 14 ~ *Jesus laid in the tomb*

ADDICTION ISSUES ~ *Forgiveness, generosity, redemption*

 MORNING PRAYER

INVITATION TO PRAYER

O Lord, open my lips and my mouth will declare your praise. Cleanse my heart of any doubt, indifference, or negative thoughts. Hear my prayer and align my will with your will so that I can delight in your ways and walk in your light. In Jesus' name. Amen.

HYMN   *This Is the Feast*

Refrain
This is the feast of victory for our God.
Alleluia, alleluia, alleluia.

Worthy is Christ the Lamb who was slain, whose
Blood set us free to be people of God.

Refrain

Power and riches and wisdom and strength, and
Honor and blessing and glory are his.

Refrain

Sing with all the people of God and
    join in the hymn of all creation:
Blessing and honor and glory and might be to God and
    the Lamb forever. Amen.

This is the feast of victory for our God,
  for the Lamb who was slain
Has begun his reign.
  Alleluia, alleluia, alleluia.

ANTIPHON   *Psalm 126:3*
The LORD has done great things for us,
  and we rejoiced.

PSALM   *Psalm 126:1–6*
When the LORD restored the fortunes of Zion,
  we were like those who dream.
Then our mouth was filled with laughter,
  and our tongue with shouts of joy;
then it was said among the nations,
  "The LORD has done great things for them."
The LORD has done great things for us,
  and we rejoiced.

Restore our fortunes, O LORD,
  like the watercourses in the [desert].
May those who sow in tears
  reap with shouts of joy.
Those who go out weeping,
  bearing the seed for sowing,
shall come home with shouts of joy,
  carrying their sheaves.

PRAYER TO CARRY WITH ME   *Psalm 126:3*
The LORD has done great things for us,
  and we rejoiced.

Mary Magdalene went and announced to the disciples,
"I have seen the Lord.…"

When it was evening on…the first day of the week, and
the doors of the house where the disciples had met were
locked…Jesus came and stood among them and said,
"Peace be with you. After he said this, he showed them his
hands and his side. Then the disciples rejoiced when they
saw the Lord. Jesus said to them again, "Peace be with you.
As the Father has sent me, so I send you." When he had said
this, he breathed on them and said to them, "Receive the
Holy Spirit."

But Thomas…one of the twelve, was not with them when
Jesus came. So the other disciples told him, "We have seen
the Lord." But he said to them, "Unless I see the mark of the
nails in his hands, and put my finger in the mark of the nails
and my hand in his side, I will not believe."

A week later his disciples were again in the house, and
Thomas was with them. Although the doors were shut, Jesus
came and stood among them and said, "Peace be with you."
Then he said to Thomas, "Put your finger here and see my
hands. Reach out your hand and put it in my side. Do not
doubt but believe." Thomas answered him, "My Lord and
my God!" Jesus said to him, "Have you believed because
you have seen me? Blessed are those who have not seen and
yet have come to believe."

RESPONSE

John 20:28

"My Lord and my God!"

The Lord's economy has been described as a "perverse ethic of vulnerability and gain through loss." We snatch life from death. In poverty we become rich.

If I lose the addiction and make myself vulnerable to thoughts and feelings I would rather bury, what will I gain? Am I willing to take a chance?

CONCLUDING PRAYER   *John 14:26–27, 15:4*

[Jesus said]…the Holy Spirit, whom the Father will send in my name, will teach you everything, and remind you of all that I have said to you. Peace I leave with you; my peace I give to you. I do not give to you as the world gives. Do not let your hearts be troubled, and do not let them be afraid. Abide in me as I abide in you. Amen.

 MIDDAY PRAYER

INVITATION TO PRAYER

O God of majesty, you took on all the forces of evil and death and conquered them. You took my sins and put them in your grave, so that I might be released from their crushing power. At times I have been enslaved by guilt, anger, desperation, sadness, and isolation, but you broke the chains of their domination and invited me, cleansed and forgiven, to a place in your kingdom. I accept that invitation, my Lord. Amen.

You are God; we praise you.
  You are the Lord; we acclaim you.
You are the Eternal Father;
  all creation worships you.

  To you all angels, all the pow'rs of heaven,
  cherubim and seraphim,
  Sing in endless praise:

Holy, holy, holy, Lord, God of power and might,
Heaven and earth are full of your glory.

  The glorious company of apostles praise you.
  The noble fellowship of prophets praise you.
  The white-robed army of martyrs praise you.
  Throughout the world the holy Church acclaims you:

Father, of majesty unbounded;
  your true and only Son, worthy
of all worship; and the Holy Spirit,
  advocate and guide.

  You Christ, are the king of glory,
  the eternal Son of the Father.
  When you became man to set us free, you did not spurn
  the Virgin's womb. You overcame the sting of death,
  And opened, the kingdom of heaven to all believers.
  You are seated at God's right hand in glory.
  We believe that you will come and be our judge.

Come, then, Lord, and help your people,
  bought with the price of your own blood,
And bring us with your saints
  to glory everlasting.

…your hand shall lead me,
    and your right hand shall hold me fast.

PSALM   *Psalm 139:1-18*

O LORD, you have searched me and known me.
You know when I sit down and when I rise up;
    you discern my thoughts from far away.
You search out my path and my lying down,
    and are acquainted with all my ways.
Even before a word is on my tongue,
    O LORD, you know it completely.
You hem me in, behind and before,
    and lay your hand upon me.
Such knowledge is too wonderful for me;
    it is so high that I cannot attain it.

Where can I go from your spirit?
    Or where can I flee from your presence?
If I ascend to heaven, you are there;
    if I make [the grave] my bed, you are there.
If I take the wings of the morning
    and settle at the farthest limits of the sea,
even there your hand shall lead me,
    and your right hand shall hold me fast.
If I say, "Surely the darkness shall cover me,
    and the light around me become night,"
even the darkness is not dark to you;
    the night is as bright as the day,
    for darkness is as light to you.

For it was you who formed my inward parts;
    you knit me together in my mother's womb.
I praise you, for I am fearfully and wonderfully made.
    Wonderful are your works;
that I know very well.
    My frame was not hidden from you,
when I was being made in secret,
    intricately woven in the depths of the earth.
Your eyes beheld my unformed substance.
In your book were written
    all the days that were formed for me,
    when none of them as yet existed.
How weighty to me are your thoughts, O God!
    How vast is the sum of them!
I try to count them—they are more than the sand;
    I come to the end—I am still with you.

PRAYER TO CARRY WITH ME   *Psalm 139:10*
…your hand shall lead me,
    and your right hand shall hold me fast.

READING   *A Fable*
There once was a man who fell into a deep hole and could
not climb out. A physician was passing by, and the man
called, "Doctor, Doctor, help me; I've fallen into this hole,
and I can't get out." The doctor wrote out a prescription,
threw it into the hole, and walked on.

Next, a priest came by and the man called, "Father,
Father, save me; I've fallen into this hole, and I can't get out."
The priest wrote out a prayer, threw it into the hole, and
walked on.

Finally, the man's friend walked by, and the man called, "Help, help, I've fallen into this hole and I can't get out." His friend immediately jumped into the hole with him. "Why did you do that? Now we're both stuck."

"No," his friend answered, "I've been down here before, and I know the way out."

RESPONSE   *Jeremiah 29:11*

For surely I know the plans I have for you, says the LORD, plans for your welfare and not for harm, to give you a future with hope.

ACTION

If I lose the addiction and make myself vulnerable to thoughts and feelings I would rather bury, what will I gain? Am I willing to take a chance?

CONCLUDING PRAYER

May the Lord bless you and keep you.
May the Lord make his face shine upon you
   and be gracious to you.
May the Lord look upon you with favor
   and give you peace.
Amen.

 EVENING PRAYER

INVITATION TO PRAYER   *Adapted from "Here I Am,*
                                 Lord" and Micah 6:8

Here I am Lord. It is I Lord. I have heard you calling in the night. I will go, Lord, if you lead me, I will hold your people in my heart.

You have told me Lord, what you require of me: do justice, love kindness, and walk humbly with my God. In the name of Jesus Christ, our Lord, I accept these commandments. Amen.

HYMN *Let There Be Peace on Earth*

Let there be peace on earth and let it begin with me.
Let there be peace on earth, the peace that was meant to be.
With God as our Father, [children] all are we;
let us walk with each other in perfect harmony.

Let peace begin with me, let this be the moment now.
With ev'ry step I take, let this be my solemn vow:
To take each moment and live each moment in peace
    eternally.
Let there be peace on earth and let it begin with me.

ANTIPHON

Let peace begin with me.

PSALM *Psalm 85:8*

Let me hear what God the LORD will speak,
    for he will speak peace to his people,
    to his faithful, to those who turn to him in their hearts.

PRAYER TO CARRY WITH ME

Let peace begin with me.

READING *Luke 15:11–18, 20–25, 29–32 (adapted)*

Jesus said, "There was a man who had two sons. The younger of them said to his father, 'Father, give me the share of the property that will belong to me.'…A few days later the younger son gathered all he had and traveled to a distant country, and there he squandered his property in dissolute living. When he had spent everything, and…began to be in need…he…hired himself out to one of the citizens of that country, who sent him…to feed the pigs. He would gladly have filled himself with the pods that the pigs were eating; and no one gave him anything. But…he said, 'How many of my father's hired hands have bread enough and to spare, but here I am dying of hunger! I will…go to my father, and…say to him, "Father, I have sinned against heaven and before you…" So he set off and went to his father. [And]… his father saw him and was filled with compassion; he ran and put his arms around him and kissed him. Then the son said…'Father, I have sinned against heaven and before you; I am no longer worthy to be called your son.' But the father said to his slaves, 'Quickly, bring out a robe—the best one— and put it on him; put a ring on his finger and sandals on his feet. And get the fatted calf and kill it, and let us eat and celebrate; for this son of mine was dead and is alive again; he was lost and is found!'

"Now his elder son…[became angry and his father began to plead with him]. But he answered his father, 'Listen! For all these years I have been working like a slave for you, and I have never disobeyed your command; yet you have never given me even a young goat so that I might celebrate with my friends. But when this son of yours came back, who has devoured your property with prostitutes, you killed the fatted calf for him!' Then the father said to him, 'Son, you are always with me, and all that is mine is yours. But we…celebrate and rejoice, because this brother of yours was dead and has come to life; he was lost and has been found.'"

RESPONSE   *Ecclesiastes 3:1*

For everything there is a season, and a time for every matter under heaven…

ACTION

If I lose the addiction and make myself vulnerable to thoughts and feelings I would rather bury, what will I gain? Am I willing to take a chance?

CONCLUDING PRAYER   *A Gaelic Blessing*

Deep peace of the running wave to you,
Deep peace of the flowing air to you,
Deep peace of the quiet earth to you,
Deep peace of the shining stars to you,
Deep peace of the gentle night to you,
Moon and stars pour their healing light on you,
Deep peace of Christ the light of the world to you,
Deep peace of Christ to you.
Amen.

JOHN RUTTER

 NIGHT PRAYER

INVITATION TO PRAYER

May the Lord bless us and keep us,
May the Lord make his face shine upon us
    and be gracious to us,
May the Lord look upon us with favor
    and grant us peace.
Amen.

O Day Full of Grace

O day full of grace that now we see
   appearing on earth's horizon,
bring light from our God that we may be
   replete with his joy this season.
God, shine for us now in this dark place;
   your name on our hearts emblazon.

For Christ bore our sins, and not his own,
   when he on the cross was hanging;
and then he arose and moved the stone,
   that we, unto him belonging,
might join with angelic hosts to raise
   our voices in endless singing.

God came to us then at Pentecost,
   His Spirit new life revealing,
that we might no more from him be lost,
   all darkness for us dispelling.
His flame will the mark of sin efface
   and bring to us all his healing.

SILENT REFLECTION ON THE DAY AND ON OURSELVES

ANTIPHON   *Psalm 121:7*

The LORD will keep you from all evil;
   he will keep your life.

PSALM   *Psalm 121*

I lift up my eyes to the hills—
   from where will my help come?
My help comes from the LORD,
   who made heaven and earth.

He will not let your foot be moved;
　he who keeps you will not slumber.
He who keeps Israel
　will neither slumber nor sleep.

The LORD is your keeper;
　the LORD is your shade at your right hand.
The sun shall not strike you by day,
　nor the moon by night.

The LORD will keep you from all evil;
　he will keep your life.
The LORD will keep
　your going out and your coming in
　from this time on and forevermore.

PRAYER TO CARRY WITH ME *Psalm 121:7*
The LORD will keep you from all evil;
　he will keep your life.

READING *Hebrews 10:12, 15–16*
But when Christ had offered for all time a single sacrifice for
sins, "he sat down at the right hand of God," and...the Holy
Spirit also testifies to us, for after saying,

"This is the covenant that I will make
　with [the Israelites]
　after those days, says the Lord:
I will put my laws in their hearts,
　and I will write them on their minds,"

he also adds,

"I will remember their sins and their lawless deeds
　no more."

Lamb of God,
   you take away the sins of the world:
have mercy on us,

Lamb of God,
   you take away the sins of the world:
have mercy on us.

Lamb of God,
   you take away the sins of the world:
grant us peace.

SILENT PRAYER FOR THE WORLD, OTHERS, AND OURSELVES

ACTION   *"Baptism's True Claim"*

The Lord's economy has been described as a "perverse ethic of vulnerability and gain through loss." We snatch life from death. In poverty we become rich.

If I lose the addiction and make myself vulnerable to thoughts and feelings I would rather bury, what will I gain? Am I willing to take a chance?

CONCLUDING PRAYER Nunc Dimittis *(Simeon's Song)*

Lord, now let your servant go in peace;
   your word has been fulfilled.
My own eyes have seen the salvation
   which you have prepared in the sight of ev'ry people:
A light to reveal you to the nations
   and the glory of your people Israel.

Glory to the Father, and to the Son, and to
   the Holy Spirit, as it was in the beginning,
   is now, and will be forever. Amen.

SOURCES AND ACKNOWLEDGMENTS*

Every effort has been made to locate and secure permission for the inclusion of all copyrighted material in this book. If any such acknowledgments have been inadvertently omitted, the publisher would apprecite receiving full information so that proper credit may be given in future editions.

INTRODUCTION

"Miracles don't cause faith," p. 1, Rumi.

"Lord of All Hopefulness" (hymn), p. 6 (v. 1), 27 (v. 1), 30 (v. 2), 32 (v. 3), 35 (v. 4). Text Jan Struther (neé Joyce Anstruther) 1901–1953. © Oxford University Press. Used by permission. All rights reserved.

"A monk was once asked," p. 6. © 1984, 2001 Esther de Waal: *Seeking God: The Way of St. Benedict.* HarperCollins UK.

"Our Lord's perverse ethic of vulnerability," p. 9. Jeannie Wylie Kellermann, quoted by Ched Myers, "Baptism's true claim," *Sojourners Magazine* July 2006, p. 27.

"Nunc Dimittis," p. 10. Copyright © Consultation on Common Texts. Used by permission of Augsburg Fortress.

DAY 1

"Morning Has Broken," p. 13. Author Eleanor Farjeon, in *The Children's Bells.* Oxford University Press. © David Higham Associates, Ltd. Used with permission.

"Each morning is a new beginning" (Concluding Prayer), pp. 16–17. Dietrich Bonhoeffer, *Meditating on the Word,* David McI. Gracie, ed., 2nd edition. Cambridge, MA: Cowley Publications, 2000, pp. 28–30.

*The author expresses sincere gratitude to the following individuals who were of great assistance in obtaining permission to use copyrighted material in this book: Judith Ahlers, Anton Armstrong, Bari Columbari, Mary Davis, Esther Diley, Linda Duffy, Sherri Feldman, Peter Finn, Gracia Grindal, Peter Hendrickson, Brian Hill, Seth Kasten, Nathan Leaf, Dan Muriello, Jeannie Musterman, Chad Pollock, Sean Scheller, Robert Scholz, Douglas van Houtin, Michael Wilt.

"Evening Prayer (Vespers)," pp. 20–21. From the *Book of Common Prayer* (1979) of the Episcopal Church USA.

"Stay With Us," p. 24. Courtesy of Gracia Grindal.

DAY 2

"Abba Moses asked" (Response), p. 29, and "God, energy, source of" (Concluding Prayer), p. 30. © 1984, 2001 Esther de Waal: *Seeking God: The Way of St. Benedict.* HarperCollins UK, p. 83.

"[Friends], you will find" (Response), p. 34. © 1984, 2001 Esther de Waal: *Seeking God: The Way of St. Benedict.* HarperCollins UK, p. 65.

"Lord, God, send peaceful sleep" (Concluding Prayer), p. 38. The English translation of the Prayer from *The Liturgy of the Hours,* © 1974 International Committee on English in the Liturgy, Inc. (ICEL). All rights reserved.

DAY 3

"Teach us, Lord" (Concluding Prayer), p. 42. © Rev. Virginia C. Thomas, in *Women's Uncommon Prayers: Our Lives Revealed, Nurtured, Celebrated,* Elizabeth Rankin Geitz, Marjorie A. Burke, Ann Smith, eds. Harrisburg, PA: Morehouse Publishing, 2000. Used with permission.

"Thy Strong Word," pp. 42–43. Text © 1969 Concordia Publishing House. Used by permission. All rights reserved.

"You Are Mine," p. 46. © 1991 by GIA Publications, Inc., 7404 S. Mason Ave., Chicago, IL 60638. www.giamusic.com. 800-442-1358. All rights reserved. Used by permission.

"Here I Am, Lord" p. 50, by Daniel L. Schutte, SJ. Text and music © 1981, OCP Publications, 5536 NE Hassalo, Portland, OR 97213. All rights reserved. Used with permission.

DAY 4

"Lo, How a Rose Is Growing," pp. 53–54. In *Lutheran Book of Worship,* © 1978 Lutheran Church in America, The American Lutheran Church, The Evangelical Lutheran Church of Canada, The Lutheran Church—Missouri Synod. Fourth printing. Minneapolis, MN: Augsburg Publishing House, 1979.

"Looking at Stars," p. 59. © 2006 by the Estate of Jane Kenyon. Reprinted from *Collected Poems* with the permission of Graywolf Press, Saint Paul, Minnesota.

"Canticle of Mary," pp. 59–60. Copyright © Consultation on Common Texts. Used by permission of Augsburg Fortress.

"Mary was able to" (Response), pp. 61–62. Adapted from an Advent homily by David Heim. Used with permission.

"Prayer makes your heart bigger" (Concluding Prayer), pp. 62–63. From *Mother Teresa: In My Own Words.* © 1996. Compiled by José Luis González-Balado. Liguori, MO: Liguori Publications, 1996, pp. 5 and 10.

"Nunc Dimittis," p. 63. Copyright © Consultation on Common Texts. Used by permission of Augsburg Fortress.

DAY 5

"Gift of Finest Wheat," pp. 67–68. Copyright permission obtained, Archdiocese of Philadelphia, 1997. All rights reserved.

"I Received the Living God," pp. 70–71. In *With One Voice: A Lutheran Resource for Worship.* © 1995. Minneapolis, MN: Augsburg Fortress. Used with permission.

"Just enough is plenty," p. 73. Barbara Diamond Goldin: *Just Enough Is Plenty.* New York: Puffin Books, Viking Penguin, 1990.

"A True Story," p. 76. Steven Linscott with Randall L. Frame: *Maximum Security,* Wheaton, IL: Crossway Books, 1994.

"Lamb of God," p. 77. By Michael Joncas from *Thanksgiving and Praise,* copyright © 1989, World Library Publications, 3708 River Road, Suite 400, Franklin Park, IL 60131-2158. www.wlpmusic.com. All rights reserved. Used by permission.

"Protect us, Lord, as we stay awake" (Concluding Prayer), p. 80. The English translation of the Antiphon from *The Liturgy of the Hours,* © 1974, International Committee on English in the Liturgy, Inc. (ICEL). All rights reserved.

DAY 6

"Ubi Caritas et Amor," p. 81. Copyright © 1978, Ateliers et Presses de Taizé, Taizé Community, France. GIA Publications, Inc., exclusive North American agent, 7404 S. Mason Ave., Chicago, IL 60638. www.giamusic.com. 800-442-1358. All rights reserved. Used by permission.

"Baptismal Canticle," p. 85, by Richard Hillert. The English translation of the Baptismal Canticle from *The Roman Missal* © 1973, International Committee on English in the Liturgy, Inc. (ICEL). All rights reserved.

"Eye Has Not Seen," pp. 87–88. Copyright © 1982, 1983 by GIA
    Publications, Inc., 7404 S. Mason Ave., Chicago, IL 60638.
    www.giamusic.com. 800-442-1358. All rights reserved. Used by
    permission.

"Let my prayer rise before you" (Psalmody for Evening Prayer), p. 90.
    From the *Book of Common Prayer* (1979) of the Episcopal Church
    USA.

"Lord God, send peaceful sleep" (Concluding Prayer), p. 92. The
    English translation of the Antiphon from *The Liturgy of the Hours*,
    © 1974, International Committee on English in the Liturgy, Inc.
    (ICEL). All rights reserved.

DAY 8

"Mothering God, You Gave Me Birth," p. 109. In *With One Voice:
    A Lutheran Resource for Worship*. Text: © 1991, Jean Janzen. Music:
    © 1995, Augsburg Fortress. Used with permission.

"On the Pulse of Morning," pp. 111–112, and pp. 167–168. From *On
    the Pulse of Morning* by Maya Angelou, copyright © 1993 by Maya
    Angelou. Used by permission of Random House, Inc.

"I Was There to Hear Your Borning Cry," pp. 115–116. John C. Ylvisa-
    ker, copyright 1985. New Generation Publishers, Inc., P.O. Box 321,
    Waverly, Iowa 50677. (319) 352-4396. All rights reserved. Used with
    permission.

"Awake, O Sleeper," p. 119. Text by F. Bland Tucker. Copyright © 1980
    Augsburg Publishing House. Used with permission of Augsburg
    Fortress. All rights reserved.

"Protect us, Lord, as we stay awake" (Concluding Prayer), p. 122. The
    English translation of the Antiphon from *The Liturgy of the Hours*,
    © 1974, International Committee on English in the Liturgy, Inc.
    (ICEL). All rights reserved.

DAY 9

"Lost in the Night," p. 123. In *Lutheran Book of Worship*, © 1978
    Lutheran Church in America, The American Lutheran Church, The
    Evangelical Lutheran Church of Canada, The Lutheran Church—
    Missouri Synod. Fourth printing. Minneapolis, MN: Augsburg
    Publishing House, 1979.

Day 10

"Your Hand, O Lord, in Days of Old," pp. 137–138. In *Lutheran Book of Worship*, © 1978 Lutheran Church in America, The American Lutheran Church, The Evangelical Lutheran Church of Canada, The Lutheran Church—Missouri Synod. Fourth printing. Minneapolis, MN: Augsburg Publishing House, 1979.

"Where Restless Crowds Are Thronging," pp. 140–141. Words: Thomas Curtis Clark. Words © 1954. Renewed 1982 The Hymn Society (admin. by Hope Publishing Co., Carol Stream, IL 60188). All rights reserved. Used by permission.

"Eternal Spirit of the Living Christ," p. 147. Words: Frank von Christierson. Words © 1974 The Hymn Society (admin. by Hope Publishing Co., Carol Stream, IL 60188). All rights reserved. Used by permission.

Day 11

"O Son of God, in Galilee," p. 151. In *Lutheran Book of Worship*, © 1978 Lutheran Church in America, The American Lutheran Church, The Evangelical Lutheran Church of Canada, The Lutheran Church—Missouri Synod. Fourth printing. Minneapolis, MN: Augsburg Publishing House, 1979.

"Lord, Save Your World," p. 154. Text: Albert F. Bayly (1893–1996), alt. © Oxford University Press. Used by permission. All rights reserved.

"A New Commandment," pp. 156–157. Text of the refrain and music by Steven R. Janco. Copyright © 1999, World Library Publications, 3708 River Road, Suite 400, Franklin Park, IL 60131-2158. www.wlpmusic.com. All rights reserved. Used by permission.

"If You but Trust in God to Guide You," pp. 159–160. In *Lutheran Book of Worship*, © 1978 Lutheran Church in America, The American Lutheran Church, The Evangelical Lutheran Church of Canada, The Lutheran Church—Missouri Synod. Fourth printing. Minneapolis, MN: Augsburg Publishing House, 1979.

"Briefly It Enters, and Briefly Speaks," pp. 161–162. © 2006 by the Estate of Jane Kenyon. Reprinted from *Collected Poems* with the permission of Graywolf Press, Saint Paul, Minnesota.

Day 12

"You Are Mine," pp. 163–165. © 1991 by GIA Publications, Inc., 7404 S. Mason Ave., Chicago, IL 60638. www.giamusic.com. 800-442-1358. All rights reserved. Used by permission.

"By the Babylonian Rivers," p. 172. In *With One Voice: A Lutheran Resource for Worship*. Text: © 1964 American Lutheran Church. Arr: © 1995 Augsburg Fortress. Used with permission.

"Let Evening Come," p. 175. © 2006 by the Estate of Jane Kenyon. Reprinted from *Collected Poems* with the permission of Graywolf Press, Saint Paul, Minnesota.

"Protect us, Lord, as we stay awake" (Concluding Prayer), p. 178. The English translation of the Antiphon from *The Liturgy of the Hours*, © 1974, International Committee on English in the Liturgy, Inc. (ICEL). All rights reserved.

DAY 13

"Be Not Afraid," p. 183. Text and music © 1981, OCP Publications, 5536 NE Hassalo, Portland, OR 97213. All rights reserved. Used with permission.

"Jesus remember me" (Antiphon), p. 187. Copyright © 1981, Ateliers et Presses de Taizé, Taizé Community, France. GIA Publications, Inc., exclusive North American agent, 7404 S. Mason Ave., Chicago, IL 60638. www.giamusic.com. 800-442-1358. All rights reserved. Used by permission.

Response, pp. 188–189. From *Mother Teresa: In My Own Words*. © 1996. Compiled by José Luis González-Balado. Liguori, MO: Liguori Publications, 1996, p. 33.

"Prayer of Confession and Forgiveness," p. 192. In *Lutheran Book of Worship*, © 1978 Lutheran Church in America, The American Lutheran Church, The Evangelical Lutheran Church of Canada, The Lutheran Church—Missouri Synod. Fourth printing. Minneapolis, MN: Augsburg Publishing House, p. 98.

DAY 14

"This Is the Feast," pp. 193–194. From *Lutheran Book of Worship*, © 1978. Used by permission of Augsburg Fortress. All rights reserved.

"The Lord's economy has" (Action), pp. 196 and 206. Jeannie Wylie Kellermann, quoted by Ched Myers, "Baptism's true claim," *Sojourners Magazine* July 2006, pp. 26–30.

"*Te Deum*," p. 197. Copyright © Consultation on Common Texts. Used by permission of Augsburg Fortress.

"Here I Am, Lord," pp. 200–201. Text and music © 1981, OCP Publications, 5536 NE Hassalo, Portland, OR 97213. All rights reserved. Used with permission.

"Let There Be Peace on Earth," p. 201. By Sy Miller and Jill Jackson. Copyright © 1955, renewed 1983, by Jan-Lee Music (ASCAP). International Copyright secured. All rights reserved. Reprinted by permission.

"A Gaelic Blessing," p. 203. By John Rutter. From Hinshaw Music.

"O Day Full of Grace," p. 204. In *Lutheran Book of Worship*, © 1978 Lutheran Church in America, The American Lutheran Church, The Evangelical Lutheran Church of Canada, The Lutheran Church—Missouri Synod. Fourth printing. Minneapolis, MN: Augsburg Publishing House, 1979.

"Lamb of God" (Response), p. 206. By Michael Joncas from *Thanksgiving and Praise*, copyright © 1989, World Library Publications, 3708 River Road, Suite 400, Franklin Park, IL 60131-2158. www.wlpmusic.com. All rights reserved. Used by permission.

"Nunc Dimittis" (Concluding Prayer), p. 206. Copyright © Consultation on Common Texts. Used by permission of Augsburg Fortress.

BIBLIOGRAPHY AND
RECOMMENDED READING

Addiction and Spirituality. Edited by Oliver J. Morgan and Merle Jordan. St. Louis, MO: Chalice Press, 1999.

Campbell, Susan. *Saying What's Real: 7 Keys to Authentic Communication and Relationship Success.* Novato, CA: New World Library, 2005.

Chittister, Joan. *Wisdom Distilled From the Daily: Living the Rule of St. Benedict Today.* San Francisco: HarperSanFrancisco, 1991.

Christmas at St. Olaf. Northfield, MN: St. Olaf Records/Augsburg Fortress, 1993–2005.

Dodes, Lance. *The Heart of Addiction.* New York: HarperCollins, 2002.

Foster, Richard J. *A Celebration of Discipline: The Path to Spiritual Growth.* San Francisco: HarperSanFrancisco, 1998.

Job, Rueben P., and Norman Shawchuck. *A Guide to Prayer for All God's People.* Nashville, TN: Upper Room Books, 1990.

Kenyon, Jane. *Otherwise: New and Selected Poems.* St. Paul, MN: Graywolf Press, 1996.

Goldin, Barbara Diamond. *Just Enough Is Plenty.* New York: Puffin Books/Viking Penguin, 1988.

The Liturgy of the Hours, Vol. II Lenten Season to Easter Season. Totowa, NJ: Catholic Book Publishing, 1976.

Lutheran Book of Worship. Minneapolis, MN: Augsburg Publishing House, and Philadelphia: Board of Publication, Lutheran Church in America, 1978 .

May, Gerald G. *Addiction and Grace : Love and Spirituality in the Healing of Addictions.* San Francisco: HarperSanFrancisco, 1988.

Mother Teresa. In My Own Words. Compiled by José Luis González-Balado. Liguori, MO: Liguori Publications, 1996.

The NIV Study Bible. New International Version. Grand Rapids, MI: Zondervan, 1985.

Norris, Kathleen. *The Cloister Walk.* New York: Riverhead Books, 1996.

Richards, M.C. *Centering: In Pottery, Poetry and the Person.* Middletown, CT: Wesleyan University, 1989.

Schwartz, Richard C. *Internal Family Systems Therapy.* New York: Guilford Press, 1995.

Seasonal Missalette Worship Resource: Quarterly Missal, March 1 to April 22, 2006. Franklin Park, IL: World Library Publications, 2006.

Tickle, Phyllis. *Shaping of a Life: A Spiritual Landscape.* Image, 2003 .

Tickle, Phyllis. *The Divine Hours: Prayers for Summertime.* New York: Random House/Doubleday, 2000.

Twerski, Abraham J. *Addictive Thinking: Understanding Self-Deception.* Minneapolis, MN: Hazelden, 1997.

de Waal, Esther. *Living With Contradiction: An Introduction to Benedictine Spirituality.* Harrisburg, PA: Morehouse Group, 1998.

de Waal, Esther. *Seeking God: The Way of St. Benedict.* Collegeville, MN: The Liturgical Press, 2001.

With One Voice: A Lutheran Resource for Worship. Minneapolis, MN: Augsburg Fortress, 1995.

Women's Uncommon Prayers. Edited by Elizabeth Rankin Geitz, Marjorie A. Burke, and Ann Smith. Harrisburg, PA: Morehouse Publishing, 2000.

ABOUT THE AUTHOR

Harriet Roberts is at the Institute of Pastoral Studies, Loyola University, Chicago, in the Pastoral Counseling program. Her primary focus is addiction, how it is related to depression, and how "addictive thinking" is transmitted through generations even when "addictive behaviors" are not apparently present. Of particular interest is the use of spiritual practice to support the process of healing and recovery.